Endorsements

"From the fires of incredible adversity, Sheila draws forth jewels of understanding. I am thankful for her God-given perspective!"
~ Alley Anderson, Founder of Risen Hearts.org

"I have been so blessed by Sheila Preston Fitzgerald and her writing. With such an amazing story of perseverance and God's grace, Sheila has made it her life's mission to share timeless truths of God's love and His healing power. She does so with laughter, tears, and a joy filled spirit. In essence, her writing is an encouragement to anyone, especially those who have journeyed through the dark shadows that life sometimes presents."
~ Chris Carpenter, Managing Editor Crossmap.com

"It would be good for one to listen to the words of this lady. She has lived it, experienced it, and knows about life in so many areas that most never have been."
~ Larry Adamson, Author *Just Some Thoughts*

"When the challenges of life are met with prayer, grit and determination, His beauty will rise again from our ashes. No one that I know exemplifies this more than Sheila."
~ JD Inman, Founder at The Farm at Bible Grove, Author, Director of Thrive

"Sheila's "Foot Notes - Adventures with Jesus" devotional captures the essence of sitting down with your wisest, funniest friend—the one who's walked through real hardship and still radiates hope. With warmth, wit, and deep faith, she shares hard-won wisdom and heartfelt encouragement to remind you that God is with you in every season. Her words don't just inspire—they uplift, comfort and empower."
~ Julie Hedenborg, Creator and Host of Award Winning *Everyday Miracles Podcast* & Christian Author

"When I read Sheila's first book, "One Foot In Heaven", my soul felt as though I was walking beside her in every step. I felt the depth of her trauma and the joy of her restoration. Sheila is an author who captures the true depth of what faith looks like when all hope looks like it's been vaporized."
~ Missy Camp Anderson, Founder *Healthy Rogue Podcast* and One Lamb Ministries

"Sheila's welcoming glow and strength of presence drew me to her. She is constant to center her conversations around Christ and His empowering grace. She may have "One Foot in Heaven" and that's exactly why she is a conduit of the Lord's mercy and grace."
~ Heidi V. White, IFOC Ordained Sr. Chaplain, LiveInThePresence.com, Synergy Bible Fellowship

"With vibrancy, Sheila connects with the desperate need for hope her audience hasn't admitted to. She embodies hope despite whatever life can throw at you. Everyone needs a dose of Sheila in their lives."
~ Dr Paula Moser Wallace, PhD, Founder Bloom In The Dark, Inc., Media Executive, Author, Speaker

"If teaching is encouraging others on their path to expressing themselves in the written word, then Sheila Preston Fitzgerald is that teacher. Sheila brings hope, laughter, heartache, and surrender to what seems to be insurmountable circumstances. Truly an inspiration, I would be excited to study under her."
~ Linda Black, Widows Ministry Leader

"Sheila Preston Fitzgerald is my personal hero. Her indomitable spirit and faith in Christ carried her through a years-long crucible of pain after an accident which took her leg. Now she pours out her faith in a new devotional, "Foot Notes–Adventures with Jesus", which is a wellspring of inspiration and encouragement."
~ Kristy Sheridan, Speaker, Author of *Third Save: Rescued from Death, Living in Joy*

"Sheila shows the love and kindness of Jesus in countless tangible ways, walking moment by moment with Jesus is evident in her life! Her testimony shines brightly in a world of despair! Along with her exceptional talent in writing, this book will impact you eternally!"
~ Hope Beryl Green, Author, Speaker, Sex Trafficking Survivor

"Foot Notes—Adventures with Jesus" is a thought-provoking, soul-stirring devotional. Sheila's personal, practical, and Holy Spirit-empowered words remind us: there's Someone greater guiding our footsteps. And His promise? Jesus is with us each step of the way, helping us love as He loves. This tender book both touches and grows the heart."
~ Maureen Miller, Author of *Gideon's Book*

"Sheila is one of the most vivacious, upbeat, enthusiastic people I've ever met. Her writing reflects this with her deep faith and trust in God, even through a life-altering near-death motorcycle accident that would devastate anyone. You will feel like you've read something from a dear friend who leaves you with abundant admiration for her tenacity and joy of life."
~ Lisa Larsen Hill, Writer, President The Network of Biblical Storytellers Int., Founder Seeds of Faith for Women

"Sheila Fitzgerald is one of the bravest women I know. She has suffered through tragedy but then turned it around to give God all the glory. She has inspired so many with her testimony and the way she lives her life. Her writing will inspire you to live the best life you can, and find your freedom! True transformation can happen and I am honored to know her."
~ Crystal Rome, Singer, Author, Host *The Unbreakable Soul Podcast*

"Sheila is as sweet and rock 'n' roll as they come. Her miraculous death-to-life story after a fatal accident, meeting Jesus face to face left her with a clear mandate: to share what she experienced at Jesus' side. Though God didn't choose to fully restore her physically after the accident—she lost a leg—it's that very loss that makes her truly rock 'n' roll in my book. It's her electric smile and contagious joy that sets her apart. And as a bonus, she is a fantastic writer! Trust me, we all have something to glean from her wisdom. enJOY!"
~ Kat Vazquez, Producer, Author, Founder *Your Story Is Not Done*

"Sheila Preston Fitzgerald is a powerful testament to unwavering faith, grace, and resilience in the face of life's hardest trials. Even after the life-altering loss of her foot, she has walked boldly in her calling, inspiring others through her journey. Her new follow-up devotional, "Foot Notes", flows beautifully from "One Foot in Heaven", offering daily encouragement rooted in Scripture and her own triumph over and through her many trials!"
~ Barbara Ann Jeter, Chair Eternal Heiress Ministries, King's Hill House of Prayer, Pray Nashville, She Leads America-TN, Pray America

FootNotes
Adventures With

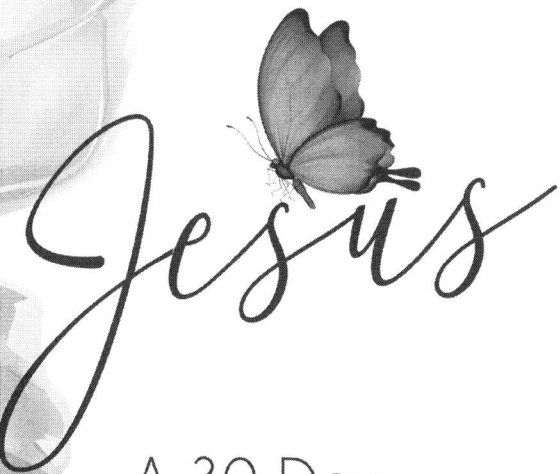

Jesus

A 30-Day Journaling Devotional
Encountering Jesus in Everyday Moments

Sheila Preston Fitzgerald

Copyright © 2025 Sheila Preston Fitzgerald
Published by Blue Butterfly Publication

Foot Notes ~ Adventures With Jesus
By Sheila Preston Fitzgerald

Editor: Earlene Wood
Formatting: Amanda Kiser, Amanda Kiser Art
Cover Design: Christine Dupre, Vida Graphic Design
Cover Photo: Brittany Allison, Measurably More Media
Stylist/Makeup Artist: Pauline Joseph
Hair Color Artist: Daniel Green, Salon Capelli

ISBN: 978-1-7333271-3-8

All rights reserved. No part of this publication may be reproduced, stored in a retrieval system, or transmitted in any form or by any means—electronic, mechanical, photocopy, recording, scanning, or other—except for brief quotations in printed reviews or articles, without the prior written permission of the author.

For information: SheilaPrestonFitzgerald.com

Unless otherwise noted, Scripture is taken from THE HOLY BIBLE, NEW KING JAMES VERSION®, NKJV® Copyright © 1982 by Thomas Nelson, Inc. All rights reserved worldwide.

Scriptures marked NIV are taken from the NEW INTERNATIONAL VERSION (NIV): Scripture taken from THE HOLY BIBLE, NEW INTERNATIONAL VERSON ®. Copyright © 1973, 1978, 1984, 2011 by Biblica, Inc.™. All rights reserved worldwide.

Disclaimer: The author and publisher have left out names and identifying details to protect the privacy of individuals. The author has tried to recreate events, locales, and conversations from the author's memory of them. In order to maintain privacy the author and publisher have in some instances left out the name and identifying details of individuals. Although the author and publisher have made every effort to make sure all information is correct at press time, the author and publisher do not assume and hereby disclaim any liability to any party for any loss, damage, or disruptions caused by stories within this book, whether such information is a result of errors or emission, accident, slander, or other cause.

At the author's request artificial intelligence (AI) was not used in the writing or the editing of this book.

this book was a gift...

to:_____

from:_____

on:_____

because:_____

Table of Contents

Preface 1

Best Date Ever 3
Judge Not 9
The Power of a Praying Heart 15
The B-I-B-L-E 21
Rewards of Remapping 27
Is This Seat Taken? 33
Life Lessons From a Little Old Lady 39
Sitting on the Sideline 45
Are You? 51
Dually 57
Faithful Friends 63
Another Day at the Beach 69
The Bridge 75
The Man Behind the Chair 81
Karlee's Smile 87
The Unexpected Waiter 93
Leftover Lesson 99
Oh Death Where is Your Sting? 105
My Mess His Message 111
Breaking Down Barriers 117
Double Blessings 123
The Quiet Engineer 129
The Weary Soul Rejoices 135
Ice Cream and a Prayer 141
The Right Wrong Number 147
A Mighty - Albeit - Tiny Healer 153
Big Hair Brave Heart 159
Hallway Heartbreak 165
Baker's Dozen 171
My Beloved Favorite 177

Conclusion   183
Practical Ways to Increase Your Salt and Light   185

Preface

Dear Reader,

You are SO loved!

When God called me to walk out the journey of One Foot in Heaven, I had no idea what that would mean or how it would affect the rest of my life. Let alone how it would affect those around me; those I knew and those I did not know—strangers who would become friends.

In 2011 my life radically changed in an instant. A near-death motorcycle accident that should have taken my life instead brought me closer to Jesus. After many years of numerous surgeries and non-stop rehab, I was finally able to walk unassisted. Because both of my legs have been rebuilt and I am a high-trauma amputee, I live life in a state of constant pain. ONLY by the grace of God am I able to live a life filled with joy.

I have learned that there is only One who is unshakeable. When every area of my life shattered: my body, my home, my marriage, my work, my mind, my heart, and my spirit, the One unchanging, always present Jesus remained. It was then that I allowed Him to become my true redeeming Savior.

Over the years God has shown me how to be more aware of those around me. I have found that He often uses our small decisions to carry out His greater plan. I am fascinated how He works in our lives, and many times we do not even recognize it. Imagine how much more we can grow when we choose to participate in His plan.

I pray that as you read the following true stories that you will discover the heart of Jesus amongst the pages. That you will have the courage to RISE UP, the wisdom to SPEAK UP, and the power to SHOW UP as God brings opportunities to be salt and light in your everyday moments. Whether around the family table, the break area at work, the school grounds, or the local market, I pray your faith in Jesus radiates in all you say and do. His presence in our lives brings harmony to our relationships. God can and does use anyone, anywhere, anytime.

Father God, may Foot Notes - Adventures with Jesus touch hearts, change lives and save souls in Jesus' mighty name!

Shining His light one step at a time,

"Be kindly affectionate to one another with brotherly love, in honor giving preference to one another."

Romans 12:10

Best Date Ever

God's Foot Notes

"Show me Your ways, O Lord; teach me Your paths. Lead me in Your truth and teach me, for You are the God of my salvation; on You I wait all the day."
Psalms 25:4-5

Author Foot Notes

As I drove home, winding through the beautiful back roads of rural Tennessee, I began to cry. I had no idea why. For me when that happens, it usually means God wants my attention and I'd best listen.

The non-audible conversation went much like this:
God: *What day is it?*
Me: *Aaaa...Wednesday.*
God: *What time is it?*
Me: (looking at the clock on the car) *Aaaa... 8:30 p.m.*
God: *Does any of that mean anything to you?*
Me: *Ummm...no, not really.*
God: *What is today's date?*
Me: *September 28th.*
God: *Is it coming together for you?*
Me: *Oh, my gosh! YES!*

Tears ran down my face as I realized that the next day would mark eleven years since the accident that forever changed my life. The tears continued to fall as I spent the remainder of my drive home in conversation with the Lord. The last thing He spoke to my heart was, *I have got something special for you tomorrow.* My heart leapt as I realized I had completely forgotten about the anniversary of the accident. God never did.

I awoke the next morning earlier than normal as I had an extremely long workday ahead of me. As I drove to the salon, I felt an anxiousness in my heart - a happy excitement. I arrived early to work and enjoyed the quiet time as I prepared for a long day. I had a few minutes to spare, and as I often do, I prayed. My heart flip-flopped when another non-audible conversation transpired. That time, it was Jesus speaking to my heart.

Jesus: *I would like to have a date with you.*
Me: *Really?*
Jesus: *Yes. Meet me tonight, 8:30 at the scene.*
Me: Knowing exactly what He meant by "the scene" I replied, okay!

It was short. It was sweet. And I was super excited. For the next fourteen hours I repeatedly told myself, "I have a date with Jesus tonight!"

I shared my early-morning invitation with a couple of clients. They too were excited for me. One was particularly cute. As she handed me a box of tissues she said, "You might need these tonight."

When my workday was finally complete, I pulled up to the "T" intersection at exactly 8:30 p.m. Oddly, there wasn't a single car in sight. Weird. When the red light turned green, I drove through the intersection and found a place to park in a small alcove that faced the scene of the accident. I wasn't sure what to do so I began with a prayer of thanksgiving. The tears fell as I thanked God for never leaving my side. Though the suffering has yet to cease, and it may never cease this side of Heaven, I thanked God for giving me the strength to endure.

> *The tears fell as I thanked God for never leaving my side.*

It got really quiet as I continued to sit in my car in the dark watching car after car go through the intersection. Again, I felt the non-audible voice speak to my heart: *I want you to see what happened the night of the accident through MY eyes.*

Little by little, step by step, Jesus slowly took me through the events of what happened the night of the accident. *See that car? They turned that way. And that one? They didn't see you at all.* I watched cars move through the intersection as every detail of my accident played out before me. I watched as my body was crushed and thrown into the air like a rag doll and then came crashing down onto the pavement. A deputy sheriff's car sat at the red light as Jesus continued walking me through the night of the accident. He allowed me to see the intersection full of cars and people, first responders, and emergency vehicles. It was complete chaos. It was like a real-life movie unfolding right before me. Then I saw it. The Trinity. They were there. God gently cradled me in His lap, Jesus knelt beside me, and Holy Spirit was all around me. The next thing Jesus showed me was an aerial view of the pool of blood on the pavement;

my body lying in that pool of blood - my blood.

With snot nose bubble-blowing cries, I cried out, "Why? Why did I have to see that?" *Because it was then that you fully surrendered your life to ME. Not until you were empty could I fill you with MY life-saving, life-cleansing blood.* For the first time in my life, I finally understood the power of Jesus' blood. My tears continued to fall, but they were somehow different. They were grateful, joy-filled tears.

Again, I heard Jesus speak to my heart:

Jesus: *Let's celebrate! Let's mark this moment with communion.*
Me: *Ummm... I don't have any elements for communion. All I have is a bottle of water.*
Jesus: (with a smile in His voice) *You do remember my first public miracle, yes?*
Me: *Oh, yeah! Water to wine. But I don't have any bread.*
Jesus: *Yes, you do.*
Me: *Ummm....no, I don't.*
Jesus: *Look in the side of your tote bag.*

I dug into the side pocket and pulled out a paper towel. It contained a small chunk of baguette bread. It had been such a crazy day that someone brought me a cup of soup for lunch. I had no idea they put the chunk of bread in my bag!

Did my water turn into wine? No. It didn't have to. The elements are simply symbols that represent Jesus' body that was broken and blood that was poured out for our sins on the cross.

I did not want our time to end, but I knew our date was coming to a close. I also knew I would never partake of communion the same way again. I sat there a bit longer, thanking God for choosing me. As I wiped my tears and collected the pile of used tissues, I heard it.

I looked out the front windshield of my car, and up in the night sky was a Life Flight helicopter. As it passed over, Jesus spoke to my heart, *Give me your heart, and I'll give you life.*

I surrendered once again as Jesus repeated the words He told me eleven years prior. *Don't be afraid. We've got you. You're gonna be okay.*

You don't have to experience a life-altering or tragic event to hear what Jesus has to say to you. You need only to have a willing heart asking God to teach you His ways.

Foot Notes Application   *Date:*

Are you listening to God speak to your heart?

What is He saying to you?

What is He calling you to do?

Prayer

Father God,
Thank You for never giving up on us. Thank You for Your will for our lives. May we be intentional with our ears and with our hearts as You speak to each of us. Your will be done. In Jesus' name. Amen.

Reader Foot Notes

When we encounter Jesus,

He rewrites our future.

Judge Not

God's Foot Notes

"So when they continued asking Him, He raised Himself up and said to them, "He who is without sin among you, let him throw a stone at her first.""
John 8:7

Author Foot Notes

"Welcome! My name is Danielle, and I will be taking care of you this evening," he said with overtly expressive hand gestures.

Taking in his colorful silk head wrap and the mismatched long dangling earrings, I thought to myself, *he called himself Danielle, not Daniel. This is going to be interesting.* He asked for my drink order and with great exuberance he explained the chef's specials before he bounced away.

When he returned, he noticed my service dog, Ivy, lying on the seat beside me. "Oh my! I didn't even notice you have a dog with you. S-W-W-E-E-E-E-T!" I briefly explained Ivy's service skill which inevitably brought up my limb loss. "That's crazy!" He replied as he clapped his hands and shifted his weight. "My grandfather had his leg amputated after a motorcycle accident too." A connection was made. God opened a door. A big one!

Daniel shared the entire story of his grandfather's accident. He was a pretty good story teller, complete with expressive hand signals. He spoke kindly of his grandfather's will to keep on in spite of the physical difficulty from the on-going residuals of such a life altering event.

I have lived in the South for four decades. Manners are second nature for me. Yes ma'am, no sir, and y'all are as much a part of my communication as yea, dude, and what's-up are for others. I quickly realized I had answered one of his questions with 'No

Sir.' He gave me a bit of a head tilt response but continued talking. I believe he recognized I meant no disrespect.

When Daniel brought the delicious seafood plate, I asked him, "I will be praying before I eat. Is there anything I can pray for you?" Again, with the clap of his hands and a hesitated reply, "Oh, WOW! Um...Would you pray for my sister?" "I would be honored to. "Are you sure there isn't anything I can pray for you?" With a pat to his heart and a nervous smile on his face he said, "No, not really. Everything is pretty good for me right now." "Then I'll pray a prayer of thanksgiving for all God is doing in your life," I said. He responded with a look of bewilderment, quietly thanked me, and softly walked away as I closed my eyes to pray.

> *"Love the sinner, hate the sin."*

The meal was incredible! Daniel was attentive to my needs and pleasant to talk with. Each time he returned to the table during the lovely hour and a half dinning experience, he engaged in curious conversation. From where I sat, I had a nearly full view of the restaurant and its arriving patrons. The view allowed me to observe Daniel interacting with others. I found him to be light-hearted with fellow coworkers and rather stoic with customers.

I do not believe Daniel was more comfortable being his flamboyant self around me because I affirmed and agreed with his lifestyle choice but because I chose to see the man behind the outward facade of the feminine appearance.

There is an old saying, "Love the sinner, hate the sin." There is much truth in that quote. As followers of Christ, it is vitally important that we do not push God's biblical authority on those who do not have the same knowledge of scripture as we do. Many non-believers have a pre-conceived notion that all Christians are judgmental do-gooders. I confess, when I scheduled a special dinner out as a reward for completing a huge writing project, I was not expecting an encounter with transgenderism. But God. His ways are not my ways.

When Daniel came to box-up the remaining food, I asked him to borrow a pen. I was rather embarrassed to ask. As a writer, I am never without a pen and paper. I even sleep with a notebook! Earlier that day I was on a roll writing when my pen ran out of ink. So not to lose the creative thought, I quickly grabbed the pen from my handbag. I failed to replace the pen in my bag before dinner.

Once again God used my failure for His glory. Daniel was giddy when he found out I was an author. "That's awesome! What do you write?" "Primarily non-fiction," I replied. I could see by the wrinkle between his brows he wasn't sure what that meant. "I write true stories. I also write devotionals." His lightbulb moment reply was, "Oooo.....Cool!"

While Daniel was gone boxing up the leftover meal, I located one of the small cards I keep in my wallet. On it I wrote a word of encouragement for him and his family and thanked him for his service. God put it on my heart to bless him with a generous tip - one that he would know was not normal gratuity. I tucked the extra cash, the card, and the borrowed pen in the black bill holder. Daniel brought me a brown paper bag filled with my take home goodies. He set the bag on the table. As I looked up, he was gently dancing. I sensed he was nervous. He took a deep breath, "Can I hug you?" "Of course!" I replied as I leaned towards him. With that, he bent his skinny body in half and hugged me. It began as a timid hug. However, I have learned when one asks for a hug - it really means they need a hold. I held onto the young man long enough for him to relax and fully receive the blessing of a genuine hug, but not so long that it became awkward. I departed the restaurant before he had a chance to find the blessings I left for him on the table.

On the drive back to the condo, the sun was setting over the ocean. I prayed again for Daniel, his sister, and his grandfather. I was reminded of my past sin of legalistic judgment towards others. When the old me encountered hurting, lost souls like Daniel, I would have asked for a different server or left the restaurant. I thank God He has softened my heart and helped me to see we are all broken and that the greatest way to share the Gospel is to be the gospel in action. I never once affirmed the young man's choice but allowed the Holy Spirit to lovingly bring Jesus into every aspect of our time together.

May we all learn to shine the light of Jesus...especially when it is difficult to do so.

Foot Notes Application   *Date:*

How have you judged others?

How can you practice *Love the sinner, hate the sin?*

If you find it difficult to serve those who are different from you, why do you think that is?

Prayer
Heavenly Father,
Thank You for your mercy in forgiving us when we deserve Your judgment. Help us to give that same mercy to others and to love those who are lost and lead astray.
In Jesus' mighty name. Amen.

Reader Foot Notes

The greatest way to share the gospel is to be the gospel in action.

The Power of a Praying Heart

God's Foot Notes

"Be anxious for nothing, but in everything by prayer and supplication, with thanksgiving, let your requests be made known to God."
Philippians 4:6

Author Foot Notes

I had heard about *Crusade: The Musical* - based on the life of Billy Graham and was fortunate to get a couple of tickets to one of the few remaining sold-out shows. Never having been to the unique location of the Performing Arts building, I grabbed a friend who is always up for an adventure.

We had a few minutes before the scheduled show time. My friend read through the playbill as I visited with familiar faces in the growing crowd. I got back to my seat just as the lights flickered indicating the performance was about to start. My friend, originally having no idea what the show was about, said she knew a couple of the cast members from years past. I, on the other hand, had not taken the time to read the program or review the cast list before the musical started.

I knew the production was about the life of evangelist Billy Graham. I also knew it was a musical and had heard the music was powerful. I was not, however, prepared for what happened next. The impact was life-changing. A male actor dressed as a military soldier appeared on the small stage. As I watched the young soldier on stage, a heaviness hit my heart so forcefully that I began questioning myself if I was all right. There was an indescribable tug in my heart as I watched and listened to the soldier. So weird! *What is this, Lord? Are You trying to tell me something? Something about a soldier? Something about an angry young man? What, Lord?*

The actor burst into song with, "I didn't know my heart could beat like this..." I couldn't help myself. Tears started to fall. *Oh God, why am I feeling every beat of this young man's heart? What is it about the song? Is it the actor? Is it the role he is playing?* My tears continued to fall as the soldier belted out the chorus with heightened emotion singing; "I know someone must be praying..."

There were many more lyrics, but certain lines hit straight to my heart. His hand patted his heart to the beat of the playing drums, as he sang, "I'm gonna be okay...I can feel it. I believe it!" I was moved beyond words. Yet, I still didn't know why. The song was over, the scene ended, and I got myself together thanks to the tissues in my handbag.

There were a dozen or more actors in the play and several scenes throughout the night's performance. From start to finish, and every line in between, the show was amazing! Yet every time the soldier was on stage, my heart ached. There was no explanation.

During one of the later scenes, someone brought out a couple of stools and placed them in the aisle beside me. My first instinct was, "Oh gosh! I hope they don't trip on my prosthetic." The next thing I knew, the soldier and his stage wife snuck out from behind the black curtain and took their places on the stools beside me. Being the professional actor that he was, the soldier never looked my way. The ache in my heart turned into the strongest desire to hug this young man. Not just hug but hold him like a mama does a child. Again it made no sense to me. It was a deeply moving scene and a life-changing moment in the story for the soldier which caused more tears, and more tissues for me.

What is this, Lord?

When the final scene ended with a well-deserved standing ovation, I remained baffled by the heart-moving experience. I had to meet him. I wasn't sure how, but I had to meet the young man behind the uniform. After the show, several cast members meandered about near the stage interacting with the audience. The soldier, however, was no where in sight.

I felt a touch on my shoulder, and looked up to see a sweet friend. "What'd you think? Did you enjoy it?" she asked. "Oh my! SO good!" I replied. Trusting my friend I shared with her my 'heart' felt moments regarding the soldier. A look of shock and surprise filled her face as I told her about my strange, surreal experience. Looking a bit pale, but with a beautiful smile on her face, she said, "Sheila, do you know why? Several years ago you prayed for him when he had major heart surgeries. When we thought we were going to lose him, you prayed for our son. The soldier is our son."

WHOA! WHAT?! WOW! Now it all made sense to me. It wasn't the soldier or the man with PTSD or the alcoholic portrayed by the actor. It was the heart—a heart that I remember fervently praying for. The heart of a young man I'd never met or even seen. At the time all I knew was that he was the son of a couple I went to church with and that the situation was extremely grave. It was a long, difficult season for him and his family. This is something I personally know all too well.

She and I embraced as tears puddled up once again. With her help I was finally able to 'hold' the young man whose heart I had faithfully prayed for years before. When the bond ended, he said to me, "Ya know, we're trained not to look at the audience, but I was drawn to you. It may have been the halo of your hair that first caught my attention, but I knew there was something. Now I know why." We hugged one last time.

Rarely do we get a chance to see how God moves when we intercede in prayer for others, especially for those we don't know. It's important to learn—to know—that God is always at work. He hears our prayers. He answers our prayers. He may not answer them the way we want or expect them to be answered, but that's okay because that's where faith and trust in Him are cultivated!

My advice...Pray! Pray anyway. Pray for those you may never meet.

Foot Notes Application   Date:

Are you allowing the power of God to work in your life through prayer?

Are your prayers filled with gratitude to God, or mostly filled with wants and desires?

How can you put into practice an intercessory (praying for others) prayer life?

Prayer

Father God,
Thank You for the gift of prayer. Thank You for the beautiful blessing of verbal communion with You. Lord, may we never take it for granted, and may we spend regular, daily time in prayer with You until it not only becomes second nature, but that it also becomes our first choice. In Jesus' name. Amen.

Reader Foot Notes

May my soul pray as my body breathes.

The B-I-B-L-E

God's Foot Notes

"The grass withers, the flower fades, but the word of our God stands forever."
Isaiah 40:8

Author Foot Notes

I was gifted a week stay in a stunning, five-star resort in sunny Scottsdale. My earth-suit craves sunshine, and I could not wait to spend an uninterrupted week writing in the gloriously sunny state of Arizona. The condo was perfect! Fully accessible and complete with a beautiful, oversized balcony filled with comfy sofas. A perfect place for written words to flow.

Once I unpacked, I grabbed my Bible, a notebook, and a couple of pens. Adorned with sunscreen and sunglasses, I ventured out to the patio to work on my latest writing project. I am a rare, old school author who writes her first draft via pen and paper. For me, writing via technology distracts my creative juices anytime the device highlights, underlines, beeps or rewrites what I have just typed. There is something about pouring one's heart out onto a blank piece of paper. Seeing the story come to life by the stroke of a pen is exhilarating!

It did not take long before I traded my sunglasses for clear readers. I also found I needed a sweater. *Burr. Why is it so cold? Where is the sun?* Looking up in the sky, I saw the sun shining brightly. Just not on my balcony. I did a visual survey of the resort and noticed that none of the balconies were in the sunshine. Apparently due to the extreme desert heat, the resort was designed so the balconies would be in the shade. Clever, but not to my liking especially in the late October season.

Not to be derailed by a smart engineer, my where-there-is-a-will-there-is-a-way mentality took over. It did not take long for me to discover the many sunlight seating options in the various common areas around the resort grounds. Knowing it would be a far walk for me, I made sure to pack plenty of water and a snack or two along with writing and research materials.

I felt like Goldilocks as I hobbled about trying different table and seating options. One seat was too high as my prosthetic felt like it was pulling my hip out of socket. Another chair was too low that I nearly needed a lift to climb out of it. Finally I found a small four seat table with chairs that accommodated my unique physical needs. The table was near a beautiful water and rock wall feature. The soothing sound was music to my ears and calming to my spirit.

"I saw your Bible and was drawn to it."

I quickly set up my work space. Before picking up a pen, I began with a prayer. I thanked God for the gift of written words and asked Him to bless every page, every sentence, and every word with His Holy Spirit. I often tell folks that I hold the pen while God wiggles it.

It wasn't long before my little writing station became a stopping point for guests passing by. Within the first hour there were five people who were drawn to the table. *Lord, I'm never going to get any work done. Would You please help me out here?* Isn't it funny how God's help usually looks very different than what our desired and expectant help looks like? His help turned out to be more beautiful than I could ever imagine.

There were a couple of folks who took a break at my table on more than one occasion during my week stay. One of the them was an adorable petite lady. Before she spoke a word the first day she stopped by, I could see she carried the weight of the world on her shoulders. She shared with me that the love of her life, her beloved husband, was slowly dying from Alzheimer's disease. Everyday her heart would break a little more as he faded further and further away. And, yet, daily there were glimmers of hope when he acted like he did when they first fell in love. Her husband slept a lot which allowed her to get out and walk around the resort. I was humbly honored that she made a point to include my little writing table in her foot travels.

When I would see her heading my way, I would ask God to give me the words He wanted her to hear. When she walked away after our conversation, I prayed for God to grant her and her beloved sweet blessings amidst their difficult journey. Daily, sometimes several times a day, we would have a precious time in conversation. I believe that my past experience with my father's long road of Alzheimer's helped me to empathize and encourage her in her situation.

At the end of the week, as she was preparing to leave and return home from what I later found out was their last vacation together before he passed, she graciously thanked me for taking the time to listen. I thanked her for trusting me enough to share her deepest hurts. There was one thing she said in our final conversation. "I saw your Bible and was drawn to it." I have never forgotten that.

As Christ-followers there are several outward appearances that this world recognizes as Christian. There are faith-based tattoos, cross jewelry, and hats and clothing with Christian logos or symbols. Yet, the most recognized symbol of Jesus today is God's Holy Word, the B-I-B-L-E.

The advancements in technology, though not always used for good, have many benefits. Unfortunately the watching world can not see if you have a Bible app on your device. Like old fashioned pen and paper, there is something pure about carrying a real Bible, being able to feel it's literal and spiritual weight, and the touch of the onion skin paper as you turn the pages.

Many years ago when teaching children's Sunday school, we would sing the following song:

The B-I-B-L-E.
Yes, that's the Book for me.
I stand upon the Word of God.
The B-I-B-L-E.

May the simple lyrics above gain greater gravity in your heart as your walk with Jesus grows.

Foot Notes Application   Date:

Is God's Holy Word a part of your daily life? Is it the anchor for your life?

In what ways do others see you being a Christ-follower?

How are you making time in your schedule for God's plans?

Prayer
Heavenly Father,
Thank You for Your divine Holy Word. Help us make reading and studying the Bible a daily priority in our lives so we can be equipped to serve others. In Jesus' mighty name. Amen.

Reader Foot Notes

Your life may be the only Bible some people read.

Rewards of Remapping

God's Foot Notes

"Be renewed in the spirit of your mind."
Ephesians 4:23

Author Foot Notes

Have you ever heard of brain remapping? Although it's roots trace back to biblical times, I never knew about it prior to my motorcycle accident. In layman's terms brain remapping is the brain's ability to remarkably rewire itself. There are varying techniques and degrees utilized today.

As a high trauma amputee I experience horrific phantom pains. Phantom pain is any painful sensation in a part of the human body that is no longer there. It can be as minute as a feeling of something that itches to a tingling or numbness in the missing body part.

In my world of limb loss, I routinely endure extreme phantom pain: a sudden perception that my missing limb is being smashed with a sledge hammer or an ice pic is being thrust into my foot. I have even had the tactical sensation of a razor blade slowly slicing through my missing calf. Phantom pain is weird. Creepy weird!

In the years following my amputation, I learned the modern-day scientific process of brain remapping and how to apply that process to the excruciating phantom pains. There have been seasons in my recovery where it has helped and sometimes not so much.

One area of brain remapping that has become a constant go-to for me is to teach my brain how to replace a painful feeling with a pain-free thought. When friends are with me and a phantom pain occurs, they know to immediately start telling me a random, goofy story. The story distracts my brain from the pain and in essence rewires the nerve pain to a happier thought. What has been an even greater source of brain remapping is my little service dog. She is trained to recognize and respond to my phantom pains. Her job in distracting my brain from the pain and redirecting it to her has been a huge blessing!

Many years ago God taught me His version of brain remapping. I had been dating a fellow for more than a year when suddenly and without warning he severed our relationship. I was shocked and heart broken. The man drove an odd colored pickup truck, a color I rarely saw. Wouldn't you know it! No sooner had we broke up, I saw a truck the exact same color in a parking lot along my daily work commute. For weeks as I drove by my blood would boil in angst. *God, how am I ever going to move past this if I keep having a daily reminder?* I heard God reply to my heart, *Do you love Me?* Well, of course, I do. But what does that have to do with this? I did not hear an answer.

I tried driving by the lot with the truck parked in it and not looking. The crazy colored truck was like a train wreck. I couldn't not look at it. *Hey God, can the driver of that truck maybe sell it and start driving something different?* I prayed. God spoke to my heart, *Go meet them. What?! I have no idea who they are, and I am not in the mood to look like a fool.* Day after day my conversation with the Lord was the same. He told me to meet them, and I kindly refused.

Then one day I ran out of excuses.

Then one day I ran out of excuses. I slowly drove my car into the nearly empty church parking lot. I had never been there before and was unsure of which entrance led to the office area. Feeling like a complete nincompoop, but fully trusting God, I asked to speak to whomever drove the odd colored truck. A tall, concerned-looking gentleman appeared. "Can I help you?" Introducing myself I assured him his truck was fine and that I did not hit it. "May I please share a short story with you?" I asked him. With some hesitation he replied, "Sure." I began to tell him the story of his truck and my former beau's truck being identical and how seeing his truck was a daily reminder of heartache. The man patiently listened. I briefly paused before I felt God nudging me to tell him all of the story. *Ugh! Okay. If You say so.* I told the man that the Holy Spirit moved in me that I was to meet him.

Then it happened.

The man smiled as he told me he was the pastor of the church and that he was working on his next lesson which was about Jesus replacing Peter's memories of thrice denying Him with the new memories of three times *"Do you love Me?" Oh wow! That's it!* God was teaching me the same lesson! He was remapping my brain's yucky memory of an odd colored truck to one of a kind, gentle pastor instead.

"Would you mind if I use our encounter today in my lesson on Sunday?" He asked. "No, I wouldn't mind. Anything to encourage others!" I replied.

Isn't is amazing how God works? He used my broken-hearted situation to not only teach me a valuable lesson, but also for the pastor to receive confirmation regarding his message. Who knows how many people were blessed and encouraged by the pastor's message?

In the twenty-first chapter of the book of John, we read the biblical, brain remapping account of Peter's conversation with Jesus when He asks him if he loves Him. Three times Jesus asks Peter if he loves Him. Many Bible scholars believe that by Jesus doing that, He helped Peter replace the memory of the three times he denied Jesus before His crucifixion.

Do we simply forget former memories when they are replaced by new ones? No, but we are able to focus more and more on the new memory and less and less on the former one. When those replacement memories are healthier and more joyful, we are better equipped at being salt and light to those around us.

Foot Notes Application   Date:

Have you ever replaced bad memories with newer, healthier ones? How has that worked for you?

What are some things in your life that could use some redemptive remapping?

How can brain remapping be used to shine the light of Jesus?

Prayer

Heavenly Father,
Thank You for Jesus' beautiful example of redemptive brain remapping with Peter. Help us to recognize that which needs remapping in our lives, and may we use that healing to bless and encourage others. In Jesus' mighty name. Amen.

… Reader Foot Notes

Hope moves us forward.

Is This Seat Taken?

God's Foot Notes

"This is a faithful saying, and these things I want you to affirm constantly, that those who have believed in God should be careful to maintain good works. These things are good and profitable to men."
Titus 3:8

Author Foot Notes

*Y*ou may not know this, but most people in ministry are not in it for the money. Faith-based authors like myself definitely do not share their written words to enhance their bank account. Most writers have a spouse whose career income supports them, or they work another job. Because I do not have the former, I rely on the latter. By the grace of God, my paying career allows me the opportunity to do that which I love - loving on others through words.

As a professional manicurist for nearly a quarter of a century, I am blessed to have built an incredible clientele. Because of my client's faithful loyalty, I rarely if ever have availability in my schedule to add new clients.

One day the salon receptionist where I work appeared before my station with a written message in her hand. "This lady called asking to speak to you. She would like you to call her about nail enhancement options. She is new to our area and is having a hard time finding a quality professional." All too familiar with the lady's predicament, I typically respond with, "I am so sorry, but I do not have the space in my schedule to take on a new client at this time." I am not sure if it was the plea from the receptionist or the tug on my heart telling me to call her, but I agreed to do just that.

Later that evening after a long day of holding hands and washing feet, I retrieved the note from my bag and dialed the number listed on it. I was not expecting the sweet young voice on the other end of the line. "Hi. This is Lacey." "Hi Lacey. This is Sheila. I am returning your call about nail enhancements." I barely finished the sentence before she jumped in with "Oh, thank you! I am so glad you called me back!" My intention was to offer some at-home nail care advice and be done. God had WAY bigger plans!

God had WAY bigger plans!

As Lacey shared her troubling nail care journey with me over the phone I kept telling myself *I do not have room to take on a new client right now.* Funny. Every time I would tell myself that I felt God saying, *Make room for her.* It did not feel like a request but more like an order. *Okay Lord. I do not know where I am going to squeeze her in, but I trust You.* I pulled up my online work schedule and found a place where I could add her to the end of my day. She was thrilled and super excited. Me? I was exhausted thinking about my already long day getting longer. Within seconds of ending our phone conversation she sent me a very sweet text. *Okay God. I get it. You are up to something.*

The evening of her appointment arrived. I was blown away when I discovered how young Lacey was. *She NEEDS to sit in your chair,* a still, small voice repeatedly spoke to my heart.

Lacey was adorable! She was bubbly and full of non-stop chattering. She shared her life story with me as I transformed her nails into a creative work of art. Lacey had quite a story to tell especially for one so young. She graduated college, got married, started her first big-girl job, and moved across the country from the only home and family she had ever known. Soon after relocating 2000 miles from her childhood home, her husband left her for another woman. Talk about a wagon full of hardship! I was quickly beginning to understand why God crossed our paths.

As I continued to hold her hands, our conversation went deeper. I gently asked her questions and she answered them with an unusual sense of maturity. I was not sure if her answers were her safe answers or if she was sincere in her replies. *God is she really okay, or is this a front to camouflage her repressed broken heart?*

All of a sudden Lacey was silent. Sensing her silence I continued working on her fingernails giving her time to process her next thoughts. The silent pause ticked on. I stopped what I was doing and slowly looked up. The precious, strong, confident young lady who first sat in my chair had morphed into that of a puddle of a tear falling, broken-hearted woman. I reached into my cabinet retrieving the hidden box of tissues I keep on hand for situations like that.

Offering the tissues to Lacey, it was my turn to speak. *Lord, please give me Your words for her hurting heart.* "Oh, Lacey, I am so sorry for all that you have had to bear. Most people endure many of the same things you have been through, but not usually all at the same time. You are one strong young lady! May I share with you a nugget of advice I was given many years ago?" With giant tears streaming down her porcelain face, she nodded. I began with, "Whatever you feel, feel it. If you are mad and need to scream, then scream! If you are sad and need to cry, by all means cry! If frustration is building up inside you, and you need to let it out, hit something! Preferably a pillow or punching bag rather than the wall. It is so very important to release the 'ick' inside. Do not bury it. Get it out! For me, I have learned to give it to God by praying. I also journal, which is a great way to see progress in your life when you look back at all you have overcome."

As Lacey wiped her tears, she grabbed my hand and said, "You remind me of my mom." It was my turn to get misty-eyed. "Awe, thank you. No doubt your mom would tell you that you are a treasure and that she is very proud of you." *Thank You God for working through me to bless this hurting soul.*

The Apostle Paul teaches us in the book of Titus about how we are to live in society. As those who follow Jesus, we are to devote ourselves to doing good. Doing good works can not save us, but they are indicators of our faith and love to God and others.

Foot Notes Application　　　　　　　　*Date:*

Are you eager to do for others? If not, why?

How can you serve those around you?

How can you improve your listening skills?

Prayer

Heavenly Father,
Thank You for Your encouraging words. Please teach us how to be an encouragement to others, and bring opportunities to us to do just that. In Jesus' mighty name. Amen.

Reader Foot Notes

Parenting ~ modeling a life worth repeating.

Life Lessons From a Little Old Lady

God's Foot Notes

"If we say that we have no sin, we deceive ourselves, and the truth is not in us. If we confess our sins, He is faithful and just to forgive our sins and to cleanse us from all unrighteousness."
1 John 1:8-9

Author Foot Notes

My beloved fur baby and support animal, Daisy, whom I often referred to as my "li'l sweet pea," was nothing shy of a miracle. She was always a loving little dog; truly a gift to me, and to all who knew her. She lived a long, beautiful life of over eighteen years. Up until a couple of months prior to her passing, she had superior health. But as she turned eighteen, I noticed a significant change in Daisy's energy and appetite. She and I managed the ever-changing daily quirks and sometimes nuisances of canine aging.

During the end stage of her life, her body took a hard, rapid, down-ward spiraling turn. Within nine days due to medication that was designed to help her, she went from 6.6 pounds to a mere 5 pounds. She was extremely feeble and frail. Watching her diminish so quickly is hard to explain, and even harder for others to understand unless they have been through it. She looked at me as if pleading for help. It was as if she said, *I'm not ready to leave you yet. Mom, please help me.* In that pivotal moment something changed in me. Of course, I would do everything in my power to help her, to keep her comfortable, and to allow her to finish well if you will. She let me know she was not done fighting.

I made it a top priority to love her well regardless of her limitations, difficulties, and her aroma. Yes, her aroma. After ten days of antibiotics her little body reeked! I could hardly hold her without gagging. The smell of drugs permeating out of her pores became a serious problem. My li'l Daisy needed me to hold her close. It is important to be held. We all need that hug—those hug-holdings—that go beyond obligation to one of genuine love and concern.

Even though she desperately needed a bath, I was concerned about giving her one considering her frail physical state. Being the precious dog she was, she let me lead her into the cleaning process. After placing a folded hand-towel in the kitchen sink for her to sit on, and pre-warming the water to a comfortable setting, I began to bathe her in love. She never moved. She sat, not even having the strength to shiver. In full surrender she trusted me to lovingly wash the "ick" away. In that moment with tears streaming down my face, the Lord gave me a precious image of a little old lady, wheelchair bound in a nursing home. He showed me a once stunningly beautiful lady in her youth whose body had become plump, soft, and too frail to fight. She had a face filled with wrinkles and lines. If she had had the ability to speak, she would tell fascinating stories about her life. Yet, in that glimpse, I saw her body language and the unspoken words upon her face give way to a beautiful surrender in a situation she could not control. She chose to humbly trust the caretaker, a complete stranger, to bathe her naked, frail body.

We are all sinners in need of a Savior.

As I looked through the lens of that image, into the big dark eyes of my loyal and beloved Daisy, I understood her unconditional trust in me. What a gift!

Is this not the same in our own life when we are faced with the decision to choose, or not choose, Jesus Christ as our Lord and Savior? I realized during Daisy's bath that it is the same with each of our lives. We are faced with a decision to live our lives for Jesus or not. A time comes when we realize we are reeking from our sinful behavior and bad choices. We are desperate because we can no longer stand the stench. When we can not stand to live this way any longer, we finally turn to Jesus, and He lovingly welcomes our fragile, humble, trusting surrender as He graciously cleanses and frees us from our stench of sin.

We are all sinners in need of a Savior. There is only One who can wash away our sins. His name is Jesus. The choice is ours to make. He is a gentleman. Jesus will not force Himself on anyone. The gift is free, but it is our choice to accept it or not.

Like Daisy, who trusted me because she knew me, or like the elderly woman who chose to trust the person cleansing her aged, feeble body, surrendering our will to that of another is not always an easy task. That is where wisdom and humility enter. When we seek God's will for our lives, humble ourselves and acknowledge our need for Jesus, He will answer our heart's call. It is in this moment we recognize that our true worth comes only from Him.

Many can relate to the little old lady. Others may relate to the precious gift of a faithful yet aging dog. Some may relate to the priceless freedom received when we surrender our lives to Jesus. My prayer is that your heart be pierced by both love given and received.

Foot Notes Application   *Date:*

Have you surrendered your life completely to Jesus as your Lord and Savior?

If not, what is stopping you?

In what areas of your life do you need to ask Jesus to cleanse you anew?

Prayer

Heavenly Father,
Thank You for the lessons You have taught us through our beloved pets. Thank You for sending Your Son, Jesus Christ, as our Savior. May we choose to follow Him in all we say and do. In Jesus' mighty name. Amen.

Reader Foot Notes

Sometimes it is only in our suffering that we are finally drawn to Jesus.

Sitting on the Sideline

God's Foot Notes

"If we live in the Spirit, let us also walk in the Spirit."
Galatians 5:25

Author Foot Notes

It was a gorgeous, sunny day for an antique car show. The massive parking lot was filled to overflowing with every make and model of mint condition automobiles from the early to late nineteen hundreds.

We arrived a few minutes before the posted opening time. My friend and I exited my car slowly taking in the activity before us. Car owners of every age, though most were retirees, were completing their final wipe downs on their show cars with pride and precision. Because it was such a large event I needed to use my scooter, Zippy, to maneuver around the grounds.

We decided to go up and down the rows of cars beginning with the far side and making our way back. I scooted along at turtle speed as we perused aisle after aisle of stunning car showmanship. We would stop for close-up visits with some of our favorites. The auto owners were a delight and more than happy to share stories about themselves and their beloved collector automobiles. Occasionally we would hear the hum of the engine of an old classic, as well as the thump-thump-thump roar of an old muscle car. My heart smiled at both.

We were nearing the last row of cars on display when I felt the nudge of the Holy Spirit. That still small voice urging me to detour from my plan. *Really? Now? But I'm tired and want to finish the last aisle so I can go home and put my legs up.* I admit, I was not happy about the unexpected deviation and the required odd turn of Zippy toward the vacant area across the parking lot. In the distance I saw one lone pickup truck, with a man sitting on the downed tailgate and a rather large dog lying next to the man. *Okay Lord. I'm going, but what on earth am I supposed to say to him?* By all indications the man chose to be by himself. Who am I to interrupt him?

As I slowly motored my way across the open stretch of parking lot, my dear friend noticed I had, once again, made an unscheduled stop. Having been through other similar experiences, my friend knows it is part of God's calling on my life; random encounters with Jesus. She caught up to me about the time the man realized we were obviously headed in his direction.

"All I feel is numb."

Most of the time when the Holy Spirit stirs me, I have no problem speaking straight from the heart. For some reason, I sensed the "Hi, how are you? God sent me to you," approach would be too much for this lone fellow. In that moment God spoke to my heart, *You like dogs, don't you? Start there.* My mind answered, *Okay I can do that.*

"Your dog is beautiful! What's it's name?" I asked. "Thanks. This is Cosmo," he softly replied. I swiveled toward the dog and introduced myself. "Hi Cosmo. I'm Sheila. Nice to meet you." Turning to the owner, "What's your name?" His one word answer, "John" held little inflection. At first I thought the man was a shy wallflower. Although polite and kind he did not appear interested in engaging any conversation.

I was tired. My body was tired, and all I wanted to do was check the box *done* for Jesus and go home. Isn't that how many of us respond to Jesus' calling? Church - check! Tithe - check! Pray occasionally - check! God was teaching me a lesson. He was not done. His calling on my life in that moment was way beyond simply checking a box. The quiet man before me needed to see Jesus, and God called me to be His messenger.

The teeth-pulling conversation resumed when I asked, "Are you here for the car show?" "Yeah, I guess so," he replied. I sensed there was more to the story. Way more! I have learned the importance of being quiet, especially when it involves heart matters. "A friend told me I needed to get out of the house," John said. I responded with a silent affirmative head nod. His hand never leaving his beloved Cosmo, John continued. "My wife left me. Marriage was everything to me. I had no idea. She has already filed for divorce. I don't know what to do. All I feel is numb." His sentences were short, and as broken as his heart. My friend and I glanced at each other. We too, were heart broken for him.

John shared several more details and thoughts about his broken relationship with us. My friend and I inserted positive encouragement when appropriate. All too soon John finished sharing what he needed to speak words to. I asked him if we could pray for him. I am not sure if he was too numb to say no or too shocked that strangers would want to do that for him, but he gave a slight nod of his head. I do not remember the words of the prayer for John and his marriage. What I do remember is that the Holy Spirit-led prayer must have been filled with words that John needed to hear. John's face shined brighter as he genuinely thanked us for taking the time to visit him.

Before I scootered away, we invited John to a couple other upcoming car events. Like his friend who encouraged him to get out of the house, I also know the potential power of the devil when it comes to on-going isolation.

Scripture tells us not to squelch the Holy Spirit but rather walk in the Spirit. Nowhere does it say it is easy, nor is it always convenient. When we study biblical characters, we find that being a committed and obedient follower of Jesus Christ is *anything* but easy. Many of the first century Christians suffered great persecution for their faith from prison, to beatings, to beheadings. While there is still horrific persecution against Christians around the world today, most Westerners have never experienced it.

What are we afraid of? People making fun of us, getting mad, or not liking us? I submit to you the eternal salvation of others is worth the risk.

May you live a life of loving others by surrendering your will for God's and allow the power of the Holy Spirit to move in you.

Foot Notes Application   Date:

How can you increase the awareness of others in your daily life?

How can you encourage a stranger in need?

What is a short, simple prayer you can pray for one who is hurting?

Prayer

Heavenly Father,
Thank You for choosing us to be Your light to those who are lost and hurting. Help us to be aware of those in need, to prepare us, and to be obedient to Your calling. In Jesus' mighty name. Amen.

Reader Foot Notes

Sometimes God has to allow our hearts to break so He can reach our souls.

Are You?

God's Foot Notes

"Be hospitable to one another without grumbling. As each one has received a gift, minister it to one another, as good stewards of the manifold grace of God."
I Peter 4:9-10

Author Foot Notes

One of the first public Jesus encounters I experienced happened shortly after becoming an amputee. I was such a rookie! I was a rookie as an amputee and definitely a rookie at recognizing Jesus moments, especially those involving complete strangers. Over time and with on-going trust in Jesus, I have learned to put my faith in Him as He leads me through life-changing encounters with people I have never met before. It is truly an honor that God chose me to humbly, not to mention wobbly, journey with one foot in heaven.

A friend and I were working on some handicap accessible modifications in my new home. The various changes required several trips to the local home improvement store. On one particular trip we spent what seemed like hours in the plumbing section. Thanks to my dad, I am fairly savvy in regard to most things involving home maintenance, but plumbing, however, is not my specialty. I was determined to conquer the project or give it my all in trying.

I rode on the store's electric scooter as my friend walked beside me. When we reached the plumbing section, we separated from one another as we each sought random items on our shopping list. I slowly rolled down the aisle of the faucet fixtures concentrating on finding one particular part. For anyone who has not been down a plumbing aisle lately, there are a TON of pieces and parts. Since I was still in the early stages of recovery, I was taking several medications that made it difficult for me to focus. I felt like I was in the land of bizarre *Lego* pieces—way too many to choose from—and they were all white!

Wanting to be successful in finding the specific part we needed, I ignored everything and everyone around me in order to focus on the task at hand.

I heard a voice behind me say, "Are you Sheila?"

Partly because I was hyper-focused on the gazillion plumbing pieces in front of me and partly because I had not yet learned how to handle the unique calling on my life, I mischievously replied, "May-be."

A young woman, her husband, and their two children came around the electric scooter to face me. As she looked at me and then to her husband she said, "Oh! My! Gosh! Honey, I can't believe it! This is the lady I've been telling you about! The one who had that horrible motorcycle accident."

> *You have no idea the lives you're touching.*

I had no idea who these people were or how they knew my story. To be honest, I was a bit overwhelmed. The woman enthusiastically shared how she knew me.

"My mom's co-worker goes to church with someone who knows you." *What did she just say?* In her excitement, she also rattled off names and places so fast my head was spinning. With my on-going brain fog, I had no idea what she had just said.

"Honey, I am so sorry, but with all the prescription medications I take, my brain can't think as fast as you talk. Would you please start over and speak really slow for me so I can piece together your story?"

"Sure. My mom works at ABC Inc in West Tennessee. Every day one of my mom's co-workers brings a printed copy of your *Caring Bridge* blog. The co-worker puts it on the bulletin board in the lunch room to encourage others and to remind people to pray for you. When they take down the older blogs, they give them to my mom. My mom brings them to me so I can read them. That is how I know all about you!"

This lady knew more about my recovery than I did. She was precious as she continued to ramble on about me, her mom, herself, and all the others she had told about my story. I finally got a word in just long enough to find out that her name was Sarah. Sarah and her family lived more than two hours away.

"Don't y'all have a home improvement store in your town?" I asked.

"Yes, but they were out of what we need, and this was the closest location that had it in stock," she replied. "What are the chances that we would meet you? I can't wait to tell my mom!"

Sarah's husband, a rugged manly-man, quickly found the part I had been looking for. As he handed me the item, I thanked him for his help as Sarah continued to speak kind and encouraging words to me. "Please keep writing, keep sharing - you have no idea the lives you're touching."

With a grateful, humble heart I slowly turned the electric scooter around so I could find my friend. To my surprise there he stood! He had been a few feet away from this unexpected encounter and had heard almost every word.

"Did you know them?" He asked.

"No, we just met," I replied.

As we made our way to the front of the store, I shared the rest of the conversation I had had with Sarah..

"God's funny!" My friend said.

"How's that?" I asked.

"Only He could create such a meeting."

Foot Notes Application   Date:

Are you looking for unexpected encounters with Jesus?

In what areas of your life is God asking you to trust Him?

How can you tangibly be the hands and feet of Jesus to those around you?

Prayer

Heavenly Father,
Thank You for Your plans for our lives. May we grow in faith as we learn to trust You more with every area of our lives. May we not only run the race and finish the fight, but do it in love, radiating Your joy every step of the way. In Jesus' mighty name. Amen

Reader Foot Notes

Don't take credit for God's work.

Dually

God's Foot Notes

*"For I was hungry and you gave Me food; I was thirsty and you gave Me drink;
I was a stranger and you took Me in."*
Matthew 25:35

Author Foot Notes

An old friend who had a passion for the stage was competing in an areawide karaoke contest, and I was there to cheer him on.

I arrived a few minutes early to secure a comfortable outside seat, one that was close enough to hear the performers, yet beyond the chaotic interior crowd. Visually perusing the area, I noticed a young man standing all alone on the far side of the fenced-in patio. Beside him sat a very well-behaved mixed, border collie. The stranger and I connected via a brief glance, and I granted a smile and a quick nod of my head.

It was apparent that our connection made the young man uncomfortable as he began to fidget and walk about aimlessly. The loyal dog never left his side. Soon we were within speaking distance. Making small talk, I asked him about his dog and if he was competing in the karaoke contest. Initially his answers were short, reserved, and very cautious.

All that changed when his beloved dog left the man's side and came to me. The man was shocked! He said his dog has never left his side...ever. The dog thoroughly checked me out - spending extra time examining my prosthetic leg - and then he licked my hand in affirmation. My new canine friend, Dually, circled his owner and then quickly circled me as if giving his approval. The young man stood with his mouth agape. I sensed there was a huge burden on the man. I asked if he was okay, or if I had done something to offend him or his dog.

The young man slowly began to share his story. My heart broke as he shared a life of loss, pain, and constant fear. The once very active, outgoing young man was a product of traumatic war. His time in service to our country forever changed him. He rarely spoke, he rarely slept, he never stood with his back to a door, and he trusted no one. Why was he at the event, I asked. He didn't know why. Other than that the venue was a uniquely comfortable place for him. He could be outside and not be trapped by walls, but yet still hear live music. "Listening to good, live music is the only thing from my past I still enjoy," he told me. Unfortunately now he lived life in a constant state of fight or flight.

> *His time in service to our country forever changed him.*

We exchanged names, and Deric slowly relaxed and let his guard down just a bit as he continued to share pieces of his story over the next half hour. He shared with me that a fellow soldier encouraged him to get a dog, and what a gift Dually had become in his life. I asked how the dog got his name and what it meant. Deric said the dog's name represented a double portion gift. One, as a trusty companion, and two, as strength Deric felt he had lost because of his severe Post Traumatic Stress Disorder. As sunset approached, the man said he needed to go. I learned darkness only increased his life of torment. I also learned he walked everywhere he went. Many times ten or more miles daily.

"I don't know if Dually will stay with you, but it has gotten really crowded inside. Would you hold him while I pay my tab?" He asked. "I'd be happy to," I replied. Dually stayed by my side as I watched his owner walk around the entire perimeter of the facility in order to settle his tab. The man made a point to never be surrounded on all sides. While a clever solution for him, the reason behind it made my heart ache. I sat back down and when I did, Dually laid down at my feet. Within seconds the dog rolled onto his back in surrendered sleep. I got the sense that because of his beloved owner, Dually rarely slept well either. One paw never let go of my prosthetic, while his rhythmic breathing emitted a calming presence. He was one very unique and special canine!

When Deric returned, he thanked me for tending to his beloved Dually. We said our goodbyes, and as he turned to leave, he looked back at me one last time. With water-filled eyes he mouthed, "Thank you."

I never saw Deric or Dually again. For months I prayed for them. I prayed that God would continue to use Dually to wrap Deric around God-fearing people, that the chains of PTSD would be pulverized in Jesus' name, and that Deric would find true freedom in Jesus Christ.

No doubt God used Dually to provide comfort and peace for Deric, and to bring Deric to me, a safe place for Deric to let his guard down if only for a few minutes - a moment to relax and to breathe.

Is there something special about me that Deric felt comfortable to share his story? No. It wasn't me that brought comfort to Deric any more than it was me that brought Deric into my life in the first place. That was all God's doing.

Our job as Christ-followers is to walk in faithful obedience. We are called to look up, be aware, take our blinders off, and see the hurting world around us. When we walk in God's light, others see it and can't help but be drawn to it!

Foot Notes Application   Date:

Is your heart willing?

Do others see you as a safe place?

Are you willing to give grace and compassion to those around you?

Prayer
Father God,
Thank You for Your loving, willing heart towards us. Thank You that You are a safe place for us to land. Thank You that Your grace is more than we deserve. Lord, please help us to be aware of the needs of others and to be compassionate and kind. Prepare our hearts as You prepare opportunities for us to serve others. In Jesus' name. Amen.

Reader Foot Notes

Do good for others for nothing in return.

Faithful Friends

God's Foot Notes

"Greater love has no one than this, than to lay down one's life for his friends." Jo 15:13

Author Foot Notes

I arrived at the movie theater and with my purchased ticket and popcorn in hand. I secured a single accessible seat with no one sitting on either side of me. *Ahhh...*I thought to myself. *No conversation and no interruptions. Two hours of solitude. Just me and the big screen.*

Less than ten seconds later it began. Eeeech, eeeech, eeeech behind my right ear. *What on earth?* Neither the movie nor the previews had yet started. I was about to turn and look over my right shoulder and ask the gentleman with the giant, squeaky-soled shoe to stop rubbing it against the rail behind my head when I heard "Excuse me ma'am," from behind my left side.

Distracted by the male voice, the screeching shoe would have to wait. Swiveling in my seat to look over my left shoulder, I made contact with a fella who pointed to his left leg. He also was an amputee, and I responded with my token reply of "Welcome to the club!" as I have yet to find a better response.

Then it began. The involuntary story of woe poured from his lips. Admittedly I did not want any conversation—especially the one he was sharing. Knowing I would soon be saved by the dimming of the lights as the preview began, I listened intently as he shared his story. The man had been an amputee less than a year due to complications from a motorcycle accident. He was sporting arm-cuff crutches and not wearing a prosthetic on his residual limb. He shared with me about his on-going struggles to find a good prosthetist and how he continued to suffer with a poor-fitting prosthetic that produced constant pain when worn. A sad but common situation for many amputees. Oh, how well I knew his story!

He then asked me, "How'd you lose your leg?" In that moment I knew God was up to something, so I smiled and replied, "In a motorcycle accident." You would have thought, by the look on his face, that he had never met another person who had lost a limb due to a motorcycle accident.

God opened a door.

The man was sitting at the end of the row next to a woman and several friends who attended church with him. I had noticed the woman listened intently as he and I were talking. I handed the man one of my business cards and told him I would be happy to share some useful resources with him if he would like to contact me. The woman leaned forward in her seat and with tears of gratitude said, "You're an answer to our prayers!" Her entire countenance was filled with giddy joy! She bubbled up with excitement for her friend and God's favor in orchestrating this divine appointment.

God opened a door.

And with that, the movie started.

A couple of hours later as I exited the theater, my fellow amputee and his posse of friends waited for me in the lobby. Each one of them with grins from ear to ear blessed me by pouring out their gratitude for my willingness to help their friend.

For me it is what I do. It is what God has called me to do—to love on others with all that He has blessed me with. God has and continues to use the on-going adversity I experience as a limb loss individual to help others walk through difficult trials in their lives.

Thankfully this man was surrounded by his village of faith-filled friends. Seeing the hope and joy on their faces was priceless. Surely their hearts were moved and their faith was deepened as they watched God answer prayers on behalf of their beloved friend.

This encounter reminds me of the story of the paralytic, who because of the faith of his friends, was healed by Jesus. In the Gospel of Luke we are told that due to his paralysis a man was unable to get to Jesus for healing, but because of the faith, love and devotion of his friends, they carried him to the house where Jesus was teaching and lowered him into the room through the roof! The paralytic received the gift of miraculous healing when Jesus said to him, "Arise, take your bed and go to your house."

In our human nature we typically think, *Oh, how wonderful it would be to have friends like that!* Yet, the real heart-thought should be, *Please God, help me to be a friend like that—one who would serve, and even sacrifice, for another.*

Our faith affects others. Good or bad, what we say and what we do affects others. Talk is cheap and holds no value if our actions do not back them up. It is true, faith without works is dead.

The amputee man's friends were moved to prayer because of their friend's physical need, but through their faith—in action—God met the need of their friend. As they witnessed my opportunity to supply him with helpful resources, God was able to use the divine appointment to grow their faith in His loving provision on behalf of their friend. I love how God weaves people together at the right time, in the right place, for His purpose!

Foot Notes Application   Date:

How do your friends see Jesus in your actions, your words, and in your service to others?

How is your faith walk affecting your friends?

Can your friends rely on you for help in times of need?

Prayer

Heavenly Father,
Thank You, Lord, for the gift of friends. I pray You would surround every reader with faithful friends who would have the courage to break through a rooftop to help a friend in need. May each one of us, by trust and faith in You, lead the way in becoming that kind of friend to others. In Jesus' mighty name. Amen

Reader Foot Notes

Generosity to others breaks strongholds in our lives.

Another Day at the Beach

God's Foot Notes

"Strength and honor are her clothing."
Proverbs 31:25a

Author Foot Notes

It was a gorgeous, late spring day. The road trip from Tennessee to Florida made for a long travel day, and my body wanted nothing more than to get to the beachfront condo and rest my weary legs. But first I needed to stop by the local market and pick up some groceries for the week.

Fortunately, I knew the layout of the store well and was able to conquer my shopping list in record time. *Yes! Thank You, Lord!* No sooner had I exited the store and made my way through the pedestrian marked walkway that I heard a female's voice.

"Excuse me! Miss! Excuse Me?!"

I looked around and could not see anyone. As I approached my car, I finally connected the voice to a person. The woman was driving a large SUV and was leaning out the car window as she tried to get my attention. She wore large sunglasses, her hair was loosely piled on top of her head, and she had a kind but determined smile on her face. I placed my groceries in the back of my car and turned back to see that she was still there. For some reason she was intent on speaking to me. Silently, I prayed, *Okay Lord. You are up to something. Help me shine Your light.*

It was a warm, sunny day and my attire reflected it. I was dressed in a mid-calf sun dress and open-toed sandals. I walked closer to the woman in her car. With great exuberance she asked, "Can I take a picture of your feet, please?" Odd, I thought to myself as I replied,

"Sure." I sensed the strange encounter was leading to something more, and I was curious to find out where this story would go.

With her cell phone in one hand, she used her other hand to lift her sunglasses to take the photo. Looking at my feet she exclaimed, "You have polish on your 'pretend-leg' toe nails! Oh my! You even have a toe ring on it!" I tried hard not to laugh at her term "pretend-leg" for my prosthetic leg. I have heard it called a lot of things but never pretend. While still in her car, she asked me to step closer. *Okay God, this better be worth it,* I thought to myself as I took a step forward. That's when I saw it. With her sunglasses lifted, I was close enough to see that she clearly had been crying. I glanced into her car and noticed a bouquet of fresh flowers on the passenger seat. Then our eyes met; hers were filled with uncertainty while mine brimmed with compassion for this hurting soul.

> *Help me shine Your light.*

In the middle of a grocery store parking lot, she poured her heart out to an absolute stranger. She shared that her best friend had been battling ongoing health problems and the medical team had recommended amputation of a leg in hopes of saving her life. Through tears the tender-hearted woman confessed that she did not know what to do or what to say to encourage her distraught friend. She had prayed the night before asking God to help her know how to help her hurting friend. She woke that morning in hopeful expectation that God would instruct her on how to proceed. She cried when she said she woke with no useful advice or instruction. "My friend loves flowers. I asked God once again, *Please help me help my friend,* and THAT'S WHEN YOU CROSSED THE PARKING LOT RIGHT IN FRONT OF ME! I saw your pretend-leg and I knew everything would be okay." She went on to say that I made being an amputee not only look easy but pretty.

"Oh, honey. Being an amputee is *anything* but easy. Only by the grace of God and the incredible village of friends, family, and a gifted medical team am I able to function at all," I responded. I shared with her how important she is in her friends's life and how she will be such a huge blessing in her life whether her friend loses her leg or not. Walking beside her friend - literally or metaphorically - would be a forever cherished gift for both of them.

Our time together had come to an end as a car pulled up behind her in the parking lot aisle. Her tears turned to dancing, and her shoulders relaxed as she smiled and said, "Thank God, and thank you!"

When I got into my car, I gave thanks to God. For the first time, I got a glimpse into the life of my own friends and what they endured when I lost my limb. They, too, journeyed through heartache and grief of not knowing what to do. As I sat in my car, I thanked God for the gift of friendship and for the beautiful heart of the pretend-leg lady. I love how God can use our burdens, our pain, and our losses to help others turn their sorrow to dancing. Isn't His timing incredible? Had I been delayed in traffic with road construction that day or taken extra time in the grocery store, she and I would have never crossed paths. God not only used my prosthetic to shine His light into her situation, He used her heart, that of a beloved friend, to shine light into my life. God is so good!

There are many lessons from my encounter with the pretend-leg lady. I believe the most important is being aware of how God works in our lives. We can get so caught up in the distractions of everyday life that we fail to look up. Our devices are great in moderation, but they tend to keep us unaware of others around us. I encourage you to intentionally look around. There is a world of hurting people who need to see the light of Jesus.

You do not have to be an amputee shining a pretend-leg in order to make a positive impact in the lives of others. Simply smiling at a stranger, saying thank you, holding a door open for another, giving someone a genuine compliment, acknowledging a job well done, or sending a note of thanks are all easy ways you can make a difference.

There are clever ways to begin your journey of seeing and acknowledging others - even for the shyest person. If you are not comfortable praying out loud for the struggling restaurant server, that's okay. Instead when the bill comes, write a note of encouragement on it and leave it with their tip. For example: *You're doing a great job! We appreciate you! Praying for you!*

Foot Notes Application   Date:

How can you be more intentionally aware of others?

In what ways can you encourage those around you?

Write and practice a short prayer for the next time you meet a stranger in need.

Prayer

Father God,
Thank You for loving us. Lord, help us to be clothed in Your strength and honor so the world may see Your light - even, and especially in, our brokenness. We love You. Thank You for Your Son, our Savior. In His mighty name. Amen!

Reader Foot Notes

God, be God in my life.

The Bridge

God's Foot Notes

"If anyone thirsts, let him come to Me and drink. He who believes in Me, as the Scripture has said, out of his heart will flow rivers of living water."
John 7:37b-38

Author Foot Notes

Growing up as a child, every summer during my week at church camp, I had "my spot" on the bridge. The bridge crossed over a rushing, crystal clear Colorado mountain stream. In spite of the rapidly moving water, one could easily see through to the river bed below. The bridge was a major boundary marker for the campers. We were permitted to go to the bridge but not to cross over it. If we stepped one foot past the bridge, our parents would be called and we were immediately sent home. Years later I learned that not only was the bridge near the massive former dude ranch turned church camp property line, but also that dangerous wildlife lurked beyond the boundary lines.

As campers every morning we had a session of quiet time. Each one of us would find a quiet place to sit and be still. Be it a big rock to sit on, under the shade of a giant tree, or amongst a cluster of wild flowers, quiet time was supposed to be spent in prayer or reading the Bible. At ten years of age, sitting still and being quiet was a challenge in itself for this busy, social girl.

Knowing that quiet time was soon to start, I would make my way towards the bridge to claim my spot before anyone else did. On occasion another camper would beat me there. Fortunately there were two sides of the bridge to sit on. God always made a way for me to secure a seat where I would plop down and let my feet dangle over the edge. The first summer or two was mostly a time of tossing things into the river below. I would throw whatever I could into the water and watch it float away. Sometimes it would float away so fast I couldn't see it anymore. Other times it would get stuck on a rock or plant life. Eventually, after time and beating from the driving cold water, the object would wiggle itself loose and move on again. Then there were those random times, even in the rushing waters, it would get stuck and never move.

> *When we seek Jesus with a genuine heart, He will fill us with His living water.*

Over time the tossing of leaves, sticks, and pine needles led to reflection. I found myself more mesmerized by the rapid moving water and less engaged in throwing nature's debris into the water below. As a young child, I didn't fully understand that the Holy Spirit was moving in my heart. What I did understand was that I no longer dreaded quiet time but rather looked forward to putting my thoughts on paper. A gift that ultimately led to creative writing and journaling. Back then we did not have social media, so whatever we shared about our thoughts, ideas, etc., we put into our (locked) diaries. Rarely would we share our diaries. Not even with our closest friends.

Thirty years later I had the opportunity to once again return to that bridge - my bridge; the first place I met Jesus. The first place He pierced my heart for a love of writing. It is a memory near and dear to my heart. I go to that bridge, my bridge, a lot in my thoughts. That beautiful location in the Colorado Rocky Mountains, where God planted a wonderful gift within me, holds volumes of symbolism.

Isn't life a lot like the objects thrown into the water? There are seasons in our lives where life floats merrily along, not a care in the world. Everything seems just peachy. There are other times in life that we hit obstacles that not only hurt, but they set us back and ultimately change our path. Then there are situations in life that hit and hurt so hard we are stuck. Satan tries to tell us "It's no use. You're doomed. Your life is over. Just give up!" He is such a liar! Do not fall for his manipulative, deceiving words.

Like the water, God continues to move in our lives when we let Him. Yes, we get stuck. Sometimes for long, hard, nearly impossible seasons in our lives. I have found that many times the longer we are stuck, especially when it feels like we just keep getting beaten down over and over again, those are the seasons when God is refining us. He loves us and wants what is best for us. Sometimes what is best means a longer season in a shadowed-valley. When we seek Jesus with a genuine heart, He will fill us with His living water.

A diamond is an ugly hunk of coal until heat and constant pressure re-create it into a priceless gem. Nothing good is rarely easy. That is what makes it so valuable. Do not give up. Do not lose hope. You, my friend, may be a diamond in the rough!

My prayer for you is that regardless of where you find yourself—life rushing by, feeling like you are stuck and not moving forward, or if you are in a season of feeling beat down—that you turn to the life-giving water of Jesus Christ. Jesus said, "but whoever drinks of the water that I give him will become in him a fountain of water springing up into everlasting life." John 4:14.

Foot Notes Application   Date:

Recall a time when you felt as if you were being tossed and beaten by life's difficulties.

How did you handle it? Get through it?

How would you encourage someone who feels like they are drowning in the problems of this life?

Prayer

Heavenly Father,
Thank You for the life-giving water of Your Holy Spirit and eternal life for those who chose Your Son, Jesus Christ, as their living Savior. Thank You that You never leave us, and that Your promises are yes and amen. In Jesus' mighty name. Amen.

Reader Foot Notes

Don't stay in the boat when God is calling you to walk on the water.

The Man Behind the Chair

God's Foot Notes

"Let nothing be done through selfish ambition or conceit, but in lowliness of mind let each esteem others better than himself. Let each of you look out not only for his own interests, but also for the interests of others."
Philippians 2:3-4

Author Foot Notes

I was on a mission. My goal, to make it to the next breakout session and not to be late. The conference was packed with back-to-back classes, workshops, guest speakers, and special events. As a writer and speaker, it felt like heaven on earth for me.

In between classes I took a much needed restroom break. Unfortunately with wonky designer legs and ambulating via Zippy the scooter, the break was anything but quick. Bathroom mission completed, Zippy and I headed to our next class. In my haste I nearly ran into them when I took a corner a bit too fast. "I am so sorry. Please forgive me?" I begged of the couple before me.

The woman sitting in a wheelchair opposite me was a natural beauty. One of those ladies who did not need any makeup. Her quiet, sweet spirit radiated. "It's okay. We're pretty slow," she replied as she looked over her shoulder and smiled at the man pushing her wheelchair. Thinking our encounter was over, I started Zippy up again when I heard her say, "Actually, I'm glad we ran into each other. I wanted to ask you about your scooter. What brand is it? How do you like it?" "Oh, my goodness! Zippy has been a god send. It was a gift, and it has allowed me to do so much more than I ever expected I would be able to do as an amputee," I replied.

She asked me about my limb loss and shared with me her physical disability. She introduced me to the man behind the chair as her husband. He never spoke a word but gave a polite nod of his head. He appeared to be a man who did something physical as a career.

His tall, strong, physically fit physique defined his appearance. I noticed he never took his eyes off of his bride. My heart ached at his tender attention to her needs. *That's real love.*

I wrote the scooter information on the back of one of my business cards and handed it to her. She looked at it, then handed it to her husband. He tucked the card into the left chest pocket of his shirt and gently patted his heart. Another sweet gesture. Only once, for a brief moment, did he take his eyes off his wife and make eye contact with me. That is when I saw it. *Yes, Lord, he needs to hear Your words.*

"Sir, I want to tell you thank you. Thank you for your selfless service to your lovely wife. Thank you for honoring her, honoring your marriage, and honoring God. I know it is not easy being a care giver to a loved one - especially for a man. You are a warrior my friend. A humble servant who is willing to put the needs of your beloved before your own. Thank you for your servant's heart example. You have no idea what a treasure you are!"

He kept his head down as I spoke to him, but I could tell by his posture that he heard and received every word. His wife stretched out a hand to me, extending her gratitude. I looked up. As I did, he lifted his chin. Tears rolled down his face, and a tender smile appeared. *Thank You Lord for blessing the man behind the chair.*

After our near collision encounter we crossed paths several more times during the multi-day conference. She continued to radiate beauty as her groom pushed her chair. There was a new found joy on his face. *God You are so good!*

As an amputee I am fully aware of the importance of those willing to serve. It takes a special individual to put the needs of another ahead of his own. To not only give selflessly, but to do it with a loving, compassionate heart is no doubt a special gift from the Lord. God has and continues to bless my life with precious, servant-hearted souls. Some for a season, some for a particular reason, and a select few for a lifetime.

God You are so good!

In the early post-accident years I learned the value of acknowledging those who help. I could hand out flattering compliments without thinking. And while those flippant words of gratitude may have sounded good to the listener, I had an ulterior motive. I needed help, and I needed those helping me to be gentle and kind with my mangled body. The game worked for a season.

Several years into my recovery someone asked me, "Why are you always thanking people?" My from-the-hip response was, "Because I am grateful." That one question tossed about in my mind for weeks.

Why do I always say thank you? I read through some old journals to see if there were patterns of behavior I exhibited and what I might possibly learn from them. I discovered that while during the years of critical crisis recovery, and under the influence of heavy medications, I simply used the thank you card as a default response to everything. I am not saying there is anything wrong with being grateful. There is not. However, in the early years of my recovery it was a simple tool to meet a need. Yes I was thankful but my heart was not always genuinely grateful.

I thank God that my friend asked me why I always said thank you. The lesson I learned helps me to speak truth from the heart. There is no longer an attached agenda with the gratitude I share.

The Bible is filled with gratitude and thanksgiving. I pray God brings an opportunity to you this week for you to humbly honor and give thanks to a stranger. What a blessing it will be for both of you!

Foot Notes Application   Date:

What pattern in your behavior needs improvement?

When was the last time you selflessly served another?

Who and how can you honor someone else?

Prayer

Heavenly Father,
Thank You for Your Son Jesus and His amazing examples of honor and gratitude in Your Holy Word. Help us to be more like Him, especially with those who need it most. In Jesus' mighty name. Amen.

Reader Foot Notes

Do not judge your weakness against someone else's strength.

Karlee's Smile

God's Foot Notes

*"Do not withhold Your tender mercies from me, O Lord;
let Your loving kindness and Your truth continually preserve me."*
Psalms 40:11

Author Foot Notes

While at a writer's conference, I had the privilege to share a nugget of my testimony to a theater full of literary colleagues: editors, publishers, speakers, teachers, writers, authors, digital designers and more. God has blessed me with many opportunities to tell His story through mine. Whether young or old, male or female, large arenas or intimate gatherings, I have found that God ALWAYS shows up. What is my job? To stay out of His way!

About half-way through my public testimony, I could see riveted eyes staring back at me. Several of those eyes held tears as I shared some of the most difficult parts of my life-altering journey. Because the story of Jesus is filled with immeasurable hope, I always do my best to include His redemption in my life as a closing whenever I share my miraculous story. I know I have accomplished that goal when I look out across the audience and see tears of sorrow turn to tears of hope and joy.

There were several others at the conference who shared stories and testimonies as well. With each storyteller I sensed a growing connection to one another in the room. Each speaker shared a part of themselves with the listening crowd as they shared story after story - some challenging, many up-lifting. It was a beautiful event and my heart was blessed.

Once the program ended, I leisurely gathered my things in preparation to exit the quaint theater. I looked up to find the exit and was surprised to see several people waiting to visit with me. It always amazes me how God uses my story to touch the hearts of others. What is even more fascinating to me is the uniquely varying ways people are affected by my testimony.

I visited with several of the people, doing my best to be attentive, kind, and encouraging as one by one people shared what was on their hearts. While I visited with the group gathered around me, I noticed a beautiful young lady waiting patiently in the back. At first I wasn't certain if she was waiting for me or someone else. I could tell she had been crying and my heart ached for her though I did not yet know why.

Redeemed by His grace

The crowd thinned out, and soon I was standing face-to-face with the pretty young lady who introduced herself as Karlee. She had the heart of an angel. Then through tears she began to tell me her precious story.

Karlee had been born with extra rows of teeth which caused tremendous facial abnormalities for the first eighteen years of her life. As an adult she was finally able to undergo multiple surgeries and corrective procedures. Can you imagine the physical trauma she faced, and the emotional and mental agony she experienced as people, especially children, said cruel and thoughtless things to her? I would have never guessed that the stunningly beautiful woman standing before me sharing her ugly-duckling-turned-swan childhood trauma was real had she not shared those painful details with me.

Karlee and I had become so engrossed in our conversation that we failed to notice that everyone had left, and the room was now empty. We, nevertheless, continued our visit. I shared with her how my near-death accident had challenged every aspect of my life: physically, emotionally, mentally, relationally, and spiritually. She, too, experienced hardships in all areas of her life as a result of her tragic situation. Karlee thanked me profusely for sharing my story with what she called "authentic rawness" as she explained that most people only say what they think others want to hear.

What stood out to me about Karlee was what you could not see - the emotional scars from her journey. While no one would ever know by looking at her now, the effects of her trauma remain. That is why it is so important to find appropriate outlets to release the hurts we keep buried inside. By sharing my story, Karlee was inspired to share hers with me.

I could easily be old enough to be Karlee's mother, but that night we became sisters. We were bonded by tragedy, connected through the miraculous healing power of Jesus, and redeemed by His grace to now walk as over-comers. I have no doubt that when she is ready to share her story—via a stage, an autobiography, or one on one—Karlee's testimony will inspire the masses! I pray one day she puts her story in writing and shares it with the world.

What is your story? Are you keeping your story bottled up inside of you? Is Satan keeping you bound in chains of guilt, fear, shame, regret, or unforgiveness? In the Bible Jesus used stories to bring hope and freedom no matter what people were facing in their lives.

When Lazarus died, and his sister Mary blamed Jesus for not saving him, He did not respond with condescension or defensiveness. John 11:35 tells us *"Jesus wept."* Oh! The depth of those two words is beautiful. Jesus did not scold, judge, or appease Mary, but rather He met her right where she was—weeping in her pain.

As followers of Christ, it is not our job to "fix" others. Our job is to see others right where they are and love them. How do we do that? Most often, the best place to start is by listening. Listen to others so you know what to pray for. More importantly listen to God as He guides you toward the best way to help the lost and hurting so they can find hope and healing in Jesus.

Foot Notes Application   *Date:*

What is your story?

Are you sharing your story with others?

If you are not sharing your story, why not?

Prayer

Father God,
Thank You for Your tender mercies. Great is Your faithfulness. May we write that on our hearts and may we profess it from our lips. Give us bold courage, Lord, to share with others all that You have done in our lives. In Jesus' mighty name. Amen.

Reader Foot Notes

If faithfulness to Jesus has changed your life don't be shy about it.

The Unexpected Waiter

God's Foot Notes

*"Pleasant words are like a honeycomb,
sweetness to the soul and health to the bones."*
Proverbs 16:24

Author Foot Notes

We entered the quaint Italiano Ristorante. The intoxicating aroma of authentic Italian cuisine filled my nostrils as my eyes took in the elegant, stylish decor. The exuberant maitre d', who spoke with a heavy accent, welcomed us with a head nod and big smile. Upon confirming our reservation he led us to an outside patio. Although we were in middle America, the covered area greeted us as if we had stepped into a historic cafe in Tuscany.

The first of many waiters quickly brought a basket full of hot, fresh bread for the table, and poured water for each guest. He was good at his job: attentive, polite, made eye contact, and encouraged us to have a wonderful evening. Before he walked away, I noticed his shirt was embroidered with the name Michael. I also discovered he wore a unique pendant hanging from a simple chain about his neck.

No sooner had Michael walked away, the head waiter approached our table. She welcomed us, informed us of the specials, and took our orders.

Michael returned with our beverage order. He saw my crutches leaning behind my chair. "I am sorry. Are you okay, Miss?" He asked. I have lost count of the number of times God has used my crutches to open a door for His story. With a smile on my face I gave Michael my best elevator version of what happened in my motorcycle accident. As he listened intently, my eyes could not stop looking at the pendant on his necklace. "What kind of motorcycle were you riding?" "A 650 classic," I replied. "No way! That's the bike my girlfriend rides. I serviced it today," Michael said.

A connection was made. I knew it was time to turn the conversation to his necklace. "Please tell me about your necklace," I asked him. I knew what the pendant represented, but I was curious of his symbolism of it. He shared with us that before he enlisted in the Navy a friend gave it to him for good luck. Although he had been out of the service for several years, he said he had never taken it off. His face lit up when he talked about it. He was grateful that he returned unharmed. I mentioned to him that it is called a mezuzah, a tube or box that contains a written prayer or a blessing. It is a symbol of God's protection and favor. "Oh wow! I had no idea," he responded. I told him that seeing it would remind me to pray for him and his girlfriend.

Our lovely evening continued as the table host spoke, "It really is true. Complete strangers do tell you their stories. I have read some of the encounters you share, but to witness it first hand - it's amazing!"

Our new friend Michael spent much time at our table throughout the evening. Each visit he shared more of himself. He never indicated any specific hardship, but there was something about him. Something he wasn't sharing. I have learned the value of God's timing and that it only makes things worse when I put my plans before His. I sent up a silent prayer asking God to use me to encourage the young man.

Once dessert and coffee were consumed and the host settled the bill, he excused himself to get the car and bring it around to pick us up outside the front door.

Suddenly her eyes widened.

It was a lovely fall evening. We enjoyed the fresh air as we waited for our guest chauffeur. My back was to the restaurant door as my friend and I discussed our wonderful evening. Suddenly her eyes widened. She interrupted me mid-sentence to tell me Michael had come outside and was looking for me. Just as I completed my 6-point turn around via crutches to face the door, Michael walked up to us. Looking at me he wanted to tell me how much our conversation meant to him. Then it happened. With a sheepish hesitation he asked, "May I hug you?" That's when I knew God's plan. I do not know why the young man needed a hug, but I knew without a doubt he needed a mama's hug. A hug that says in unspoken words 'you are loved.' A hug that turns into a hold, long enough for all the broken pieces inside to melt back together.

The young man towered over me but in that moment he responded like a little boy. The healing embrace ended. When I opened my eyes and looked at my dear friend who stood by watching, I saw her mouth hanging wide open. Michael thanked us again as he made a quick return inside the restaurant. I noticed a lift of his head, and joy in his step.

My friend's husband pulled up in the car just as the heart hug ended. Once in the car my sweet friend could not stop talking about it.

What an honor it is to be used by God! To be a vessel of encouragement and hope to another. The Bible tells us in Romans 14:19 "to pursue the things which make for peace and the things by which one may edify another." You do not have to have endured hardship for God to use you. It is not your story that people are drawn to. It is your heart. I know many people who have endured horrific trauma, and they choose not to use their story for good. I also know countless others who use their life-altering situations to encourage everyone they meet. It truly depends on the heart of the individual.

God continually used, and still uses, the least likely folks to bring about His gospel message to a lost and hurting world. He's not simply looking for survivors, but a willing heart. When we are willing, God will create in us a warrior spirit! Are you willing?

Foot Notes Application

Date:

What has God helped you overcome?

How are you allowing God to use you?

How can you be better equipped to share your overcomer testimony?

Prayer

Heavenly Father,
Thank You for unexpected encounters. Help us to not only be aware of others but equip us to be Your vessels to edify those in need. In Jesus' mighty name. Amen.

Reader Foot Notes

We do not need a big platform

to make a big difference.

Leftover Lesson

God's Foot Notes

*"Trust in the Lord with all your heart, and lean not on your own understanding;
In all your ways acknowledge Him, and He shall direct your paths."*
Proverbs 3:5-6

Author Foot Notes

Are you missing out on some great opportunities because you think they are not important?
I live in a small community that borders a local fire and ambulance station which comes in handy for my neighbors as many of them are retired senior citizens. Please do not get me wrong. They are a feisty bunch even though their bodies may not allow them to put into action what their spunky selves want to do. Occasionally one of them falls, but our first responders come quickly to their rescue. Needless to say, they know my community quite well.
  Over the years a group of neighbors and I have had the honor to give back to our first responders with regular homemade meals. We create the menu, divvy up meal preparation, and deliver the tasty homemade meals to the station. On one particular occasion, I was responsible for the dessert. Since it was strawberry pickin' season, I chose to make a yummy strawberry sheet cake - a large cake that feeds a crowd, as well as being a guest favorite.
  I decided to double the recipe so it would serve our large group of hungry heroes. Everything progressed nicely in the kitchen until I poured the double batch of batter into a large foil to-go baking pan. As I poured in the batter, I realized there was about a cup and a half too much batter to fit in the pan. For a quick moment I thought to myself, *Oh, just pour it in,*

Are You sure, Lord?

it'll fit. Thank goodness wisdom kicked in from a past experience of scraping and cleaning up overflowed, caked-on food inside the oven. That horrible memory put an abrupt stop to the zealous batter pouring. Digging through the cabinet of bakeware, I found a couple of miniature loaf pans for the excess cake batter.

With the cakes in the oven and the kitchen cleaned up, I relaxed for a few minutes. That is when the questions began. *Who should I give the mini cakes to? Who did I last give a meal, soup, or dessert to? Is someone feeling down, or lonely, or not well?* A dozen questions ran through my mind, and yet my mind kept coming back to one particular neighbor. *Really? I try and love on them often. Shouldn't I be "sharing the love" to someone else?*

For the next hour while the cakes finished baking and I made the fresh strawberry icing, my mind fought against the idea of giving the mini cake to the neighbor I routinely share with. *Are You sure, Lord? Shouldn't I be blessing someone new?* Complete silence filled the air.

It was one of those silent moments reminiscent of my youth. You all know what I am talking about. That silent look on your parent's face when you have asked the same question over and over again. In that moment I felt like I had received the do not ask Me again look. Unlike with my parents, I learned that it is best not to debate God. I surrendered to His will.

After the cakes were cooled, iced, and ready for delivery, I obeyed God's instructions and took the cake to my neighbor. When she answered the door, I explained that it was a fresh, homemade strawberry cake. She gasped as she took the little dessert. I saw tears fill her eyes. While she is normally generous with her gratitude, that particular day she was overwhelmingly so.

I later found out that it was her daughter's birthday and that she had asked her mom for one thing. Yep, you guessed it, a homemade strawberry cake. While my neighbor is generally fully capable of baking a cake, she suffers with some serious health issues. There are times when her body is unable to keep up. She wanted so badly to bless her daughter on her special day. Unfortunately on that particular day my neighbor's body failed to honor the blessing she so desperately wanted to give to her daughter.

But God. God knew the need. He had a plan. Silly me, thinking I knew better than God. I do not always understand the heart-nudges from God, but if there is one thing I have learned, it is to trust Him - especially when I do not understand or agree with Him. That does not mean it is easy! Learning to trust God, like anything else, takes practice—intentional practice at that.

We often miss opportunities to love others when we get caught up in our selfish ideas.

God's plans are always better than ours.

When we lean on something or someone, we put our weight into it. When we set our minds on something or put our trust in someone without a full understanding of the thing or person, we often set ourselves up for failure. In James 1:5, Jesus' brother, tells us, *"If any of you lacks wisdom, let him ask of God, who gives liberally and without reproach, and it will be given to him."* To me the best part of that chapter is what follows in verse six; *"But let him ask in faith, with no doubting."*

Foot Notes Application   Date:

In what areas of your life can you be less self-centered and more God-centered?

How can you fully trust God with expectation?

What obstacles - that which hinder your faith in God - do you need to ask God to remove in your life?

Prayer

Heavenly Father,
Thank You, Lord, for continuing to mold and use us for Your will. Help us Lord to trust to You for wisdom and direction in our lives. May we not lean on our own understanding but on Yours. Please remove all doubt we carry regarding Your love for us. In Jesus' mighty name. Amen.

Reader Foot Notes

When God speaks...respond!

Oh Death Where is Your Sting?

God's Foot Notes

"For to me, to live is Christ, and to die is gain."
Philippians 1:21

Author Foot Notes

I am a single, childless woman of God. Most of my family members have already relocated from this earth to be with Jesus, and while I do not have grand material assets, according to this world's standards, I was raised to be responsible and accountable with the gifts that I have.

Like most folks, I was not all that excited about tackling the "final arrangements upon death" planning process. Not because I am bothered by the thought of dying, but rather because I believe the extreme expenses people pour into funeral plans aren't necessarily frugal. The way I see it, my earth suit has little to no value without the life-giving breath only God provides. Regardless of my steps to this life's ending preferences, I knew it was the responsible thing for me to handle those arrangements versus expecting one of my remaining siblings to have to do it.

I did my due diligence by researching area funeral homes. The Lord blessed me with a sweet, young advisor. Our initial conversation was over the phone. I found her to be a polite, gentle, and soft-spoken professional. She was kind to offer to meet in my home.

The day of our scheduled appointment arrived. I had done some prior research on her and found we had a few friends in common. I believed we would work well together. When she arrived, she hugged me as if we were long-lost friends. A symbol of confirmation to me that she was the one God chose for me.

We easily fell into a rhythm of friendly conversation. She told me a bit about herself, her husband, and their children. Funny, she too had done her due diligence and researched me prior to our meeting. Between my website and various links to TV shows and podcasts I have been a guest on, she knew my story fairly well.

She explained to me the various funeral package options they had available. I had already prayed and thought about what I preferred. I am definitely a girly-girl who loves a bit of bling, but it makes no sense to me to spend money on anything that is no longer useful. When my earthly body dies - outside of donating it to science - it will be of no use. I think she was a bit surprised when I told her I wanted the bare, a la carte minimum; a basic cremation with the complimentary basic urn, a complimentary online obituary notice, and the minimal number of death certificates. "What about a celebration of life?" She suggested. "I figure if folks want to gather they will. If not, that is okay. I only have two siblings and they live in distant states." "But, so many people know you. I am sure they would want to honor you if you pre-planned a celebration of life gathering. I realize you won't need it, but it would be a gift for them." She was right. I did not need to be so frugal that I would take away the opportunity for others if they needed to gather for closure. With my decisions made, she filled out forms checking boxes here and there.

With the business completed, our conversation turned back to friendly personal subject matter. She commented on how peaceful and inviting my home was. "Thank you so much! God has grown the gift of hospitality in my journey. I am so very grateful to share with others that which He has blessed me with. Especially to those who may not know how much they may need it."

We easily fell into a rhythm of friendly conversation.

"How did you get into the funeral business?" I asked. She explained the ideal logistics of the job which allowed her flexibility for her family, and the rewards that come from serving those in difficult times. I could see why the young lady was good at her job.

Her countenance changed, and she got really quiet as she sat back and relaxed on the sofa. I could see she was in deep thought. I sat patiently, giving her the opportunity to share that which was on her mind if she so chose. Slowly she shared a beautiful, deeply personal season in her life.

My heart ached as she relayed the sorrowful, life-altering details of the death of her infant son, and how that loss completely changed the trajectory of her life from what she thought it would be. Tears trickled down her face as she poured her heart out.

Sometimes there are no words. Sometimes there are no need for words. I gently took her hand. As soon as I did, her tears increased. Still holding her hand, I reached beside me, grabbed the tissues, and handed her the box. As I held this precious one's hand, God gave me a beautiful vision. The setting was Heaven, and the woman before me was entering eternal glory after a life well lived. I saw an adorable, joy-filled child running through a field of wild flowers towards the entrance to Heaven. With his arms stretched wide, he gleefully yelled to his mother, "You're here! You're finally here!" *God, am I supposed to share this with her?*

Receiving an affirmation in my heart from God, I shared the vision with her. I was not sure how she would respond. We never know how others will receive God's love for them. She held onto every word as it was oxygen to her lungs and fuel to her soul. Her tears continued to fall, but they were now tears of joy. Tears of living water. "Thank you so much for sharing that with me. You have no idea what that means to me."

Her phone beeped and it was time for her to leave. As I walked her to the door, she turned to give me a hug. Making her way out the door she continued to utter gratitude. Then it happened! Before she reached her car, she quickly ran back to me and gave me a big ol' bear hug. God is so good!

If we are honest, most people fear death. We can try to avoid it but that does not change the fact that we all will die. Only faith in Christ Jesus as our Lord and Savior can sustain us from the fear of death. When we know that this life is not the end, only then can we truly live!

Foot Notes Application

Date:

Are you afraid of death? If so, why?

In what ways can you overcome the fear of dying?

What is keeping you from truly living your life to the fullest?

Prayer

Heavenly Father,
Thank You for Jesus' blood shed on the cross for our sins and that He conquered death and the grave. Thank You that when we choose Jesus as our Lord and Savior we no longer have to fear death. In Jesus' mighty name. Amen.

Reader Foot Notes

Tears are simply liquid words.

My Mess His Message

God's Foot Notes

""Be angry, and do not sin. Do not let the sun go down on your wrath."
Ephesians 4:26

Author Foot Notes

It had been a long day—a VERY long day. It was cold outside which causes my rebuilt designer legs to ache horribly. I had just finished a ten hour work day, and I needed to make one quick stop before heading home to rest my cold, tired, and weary body.

Fortunately the large warehouse retail store wasn't too crowded. With Ivy, my new service pup in training, properly secured to my body, I mounted an electric buggy (a shopping cart for all those non-southerners) and proceeded through the entryway. With a tired smile, the store clerk asked if my dog was a service dog. I nodded and replied yes as I continued on. The clerk gently, but quickly, put up a hand for me to stop.

That was when it hit me. A decade of pent-up frustrations from that particular store nearly every time I rolled through the entryway exploded within me and poured from my lips. I am ashamed to admit my poor behavior. I unloaded a dump truck full of annoyances on her when she asked, "What service does your dog perform?" Somewhere in the middle of my angry, verbal blasting, I asked to speak to the manager. The poor woman patiently listened to me, or most likely tuned me out, and then waved me on as she said, "Do whatever you are gonna do."

I am not sure what changed in me. Maybe I subconsciously was aware that I was acting like a buffoon. Maybe it was because I routinely frequent that store, and I wanted the situation settled once and for all. Regardless, God softened my heart. Ten years is a very long time to carry "ick". For whatever reason, I asked her, "Please tell me the store's current policy on service animals because this is the only place that gives me a problem most every time I enter."

The atmosphere suddenly changed. Something in both of us shifted. No doubt, for me, it was because she maintained a professional and courteous attitude throughout our conversation. Maybe for her, she realized I finished venting my frustrations and was in a better place for open dialogue. I thank God the conversation turned to a healthy, respectful one.

Oh, the depth of chaos our choices can create!

We ironed out the store's policies making sure they were in line with Federal ADA Guidelines. It seemed that individual store leadership and employee interpretations were the cause of most of the issues. Before my conversation ended with the entry clerk, I apologized to her several times, thanking her for her grace and patience. She and I ended up having a really nice visit before I shopped.

I quickly picked up the few things I needed, and as I checked out I asked for the store manager. Not because I wanted to complain but because I wanted to acknowledge how well his employee handled a long, on-going problem. He was kind and accommodating, willing to hear my concerns. I found it interesting that even though my prosthetic was fully visible - sticking straight out from the electric buggy, and a walking cane was in the cart, he never saw it. I encouraged him to train his staff to be more observant, as that is an easy way to, not always, but many times to identify a physical disability. I shared with him that there are some folks, many military, who battle PTSD and that the drill-style situation to enter their store could easily trigger some people, causing more harm than good.

Believe me, I am fully aware that there are countless people who take advantage of the ADA service animal laws. Maybe one day there will be a genuine legal ADA registration and documentation for ADA service animals. Until then I pray the next time I am confronted with the situation, God will grant the same grace the store clerk gave me when I unfairly blasted her.

Even so, for days I felt a tug on my heart saying, *Sheila, you need to bless her for her kindness.* Within a week of my horrible behavior toward the store clerk, I put together a fresh floral arrangement along with a note of apology and gratitude. A friend helped me by delivering them to her. Interesting that by needing a friend to help with the floral delivery, I had to share my messy behavior experience with her. Oh, the depth of chaos our choices can create! Fortunately God used my mess to bless her as well.

It is okay to get frustrated or even angry. Both the old and new testaments speak to it. Psalms 4:4 and Ephesians 4:26 state, *"Be angry, and do not sin."* Which means we can be angry so long as we do not sin. Where we get in trouble is when we let anger cause sin.

Was I justified in my anger? Absolutely. Does justification merit quarreling and unkindness toward another? Absolutely not. Titus chapter three teaches that for us to live right within society we are to avoid disputes and contentions.

I thank God that He pierced my heart with regret and understanding before I rolled away from the store clerk that day. While my poopy behavior still stings my selfish pride, I am grateful God continues to remind me of His Golden Rule; *"Therefore, whatever you want men to do to you, do also to them, for this is the Law and the Prophets."* Matthew 7:12.

If you are battling anger, frustration, or unresolved conflict, I pray God softens your heart and leads you to true heart healing. This life is hard enough. We sure do not need to carry any unnecessary burdens. It really is never too late to follow up a wrong decision with a right one.

Foot Notes Application   Date:

Are you upset, frustrated, angry? If so, why?

How can anger or frustration lead you down a path of sinful, selfish thoughts and behavior?

If you have unresolved conflict with someone, how can you find resolution?

Prayer

Heavenly Father,
Thank You for loving us even when we act against Your will. Thank You for Your loving patience and guidance in helping us learn from our mistakes. May we turn away from selfish behavior and run to You. In Jesus' mighty name. Amen.

Reader Foot Notes

It is never too late to be the person God created you to be.

Breaking Down Barriers

God's Foot Notes

"Blessed be the God and Father of our Lord Jesus Christ, the Father of mercies and God of all comfort, who comforts us in all our tribulation, that we may be able to comfort those who are in any trouble, with the comfort with which we ourselves are comforted by God."
2 Corinthians 1:3-4

Author Foot Notes

"Good morning!" I heard him say in a uniquely unfamiliar accent. I looked up from my latest manuscript-in-process to see a middle-aged man dressed in a maintenance uniform. "Good mornin'! How are you today?" I replied, returning the smile he gave me.

As he got closer to where I was sitting he said, "It's a beautiful fall day! The pools are serviced and clean. I hope the water wall cooperates as nicely." His heavy accent made it difficult for my ears to process his otherwise well-spoken English. I sensed he felt the same when he tried to decipher my southern drawl. It was entertaining for both of us.

I love the sound of moving water. Be it a bubbling brook, a mountain stream, a roaring waterfall, or waves crashing along the shore. When I travel, I find great peace in their God-created symphony sound. Having secured a comfortable table next to a water wall feature, I was able to focus on writing and ignore most of the distractions around me. However, I have learned that when God brings people across my path, they are not distractions but rather part of His plan. The kind stranger with a distant language was no exception.

As he serviced the water wall feature, I learned his name was Damir, and he and his young bride immigrated to the United States via Hungary due to the war in his home country of Croatia many years ago. His story was beautifully broken. As an American who has never personally experienced war, I was intrigued by his account of his journey. Suddenly

Damir's pager went off and he abruptly ended his current story. Before he departed he asked, "How long will you be here?" "I will be here all week," I answered. With a giant grin he said, "Great! I will see you again." I was grateful for the temporary reprieve as my mind needed time to process all Damir had shared with me.

Over the next couple of days Damir divulged multiple heart-wrenching stories of his and his family's life. As I intently listened to every account, I noticed a pattern emerging. Each tragic retelling held an undercurrent of grief. So much loss in one life. Loss of the joy of being a newlywed, the loss of friends, the loss of family, and the loss of his childhood home. The loss of adventure being forced to flee his home country not knowing how or even where he and his new bride would live or how they would survive.

I thanked God that He brought Damir to my table and that He helped me to see what Damir was really trying to tell me. *Oh Lord, please give me a compassionate heart and the comforting words You want him to hear.*

"If you could go back to Croatia now, would you?" I asked him. "I have been back a few times for visits, but it is not the same. The home I knew no longer exists - neither my home nor my home country. The war destroyed the land I loved."

"Oh, Damir, I can not begin to imagine how hard that has been for you."

His story was beautifully broken.

I shared with him that while I do not know his specific grief, I do understand loss. Because of my accident, I too experienced many years of trauma and loss. Extreme loss tends to leave permanent scars; some obviously physical, while most are painfully invisible to those around us.

On the final day of my stay, Damir shyly asked if we could take a photo together. "I would be honored. Thank you for asking." He handed his phone to a co-worker, and as Damir stood beside me, he politely asked, "May I put my hand on your shoulder?" Adjusting the crutches under my arms, I moved a bit closer to him. "Thank you," he whispered. "I want to have a token of our conversations. They have meant so much to me and my wife. She tells me I am happier than I have been in a very long time." After his kind words spoken, tears puddled in my eyes as my heart smiled. *God, You are so, so good!*

We have all experienced grief and loss. Even a young child goes through the feelings of grief when they lose a favorite toy or a best buddy moves away. As we age, the column of loss in our lives usually grows with deeper heartache attached to it. In every life there are seasons of grief, and the only way to get through them is to replace the grief with comfort.

The real question is what type of comfort will you turn to in your grief? What kind of comfort will you give others who are grieving? Unfortunately too many of us turn to temporary comforts which really are not comforts at all. Things like power, wealth, sex, drugs, alcohol, and any other thing one might use when grieving is simply a camouflage for dealing with the real issue. Too many times we bury our grief under addictions or bad choices.

The Bible tells us in 1 Peter 5:6-7, *"Therefore humble yourselves under the mighty hand of God, that He may exalt you in due time, casting all your care upon Him, for He cares for you."*

Many of us have seen the "cast your cares upon Him" on t-shirts and wall decor which is great, but most fail to read the previous verse where we are told to humble ourselves before God and that His exalting of us is in *His* time - not ours.

God loves us so much. When we humbly surrender our grief to Him, and not to our circumstances, He can bring His lasting comfort to our lives. Once we have experienced the true comfort that only comes from God can we then share that comfort with others.

There are many ways to comfort someone: put yourself in their shoes, listen - do not preach or give bumper sticker responses to them, encourage rather than criticize, and most importantly show genuine concern. The best comforters are those who have learned from their own personal experiences. I encourage you to use your own learning to help comfort others as they grow in their journey of following Jesus Christ.

Foot Notes Application   *Date:*

Is there any unresolved grief in your life? If so, what is it?

What or where do you go for comfort?

Who do you know who is grieving? How can you comfort them?

Prayer

Heavenly Father,
Thank You for Your endless comfort. Help us to turn to You for comfort and to turn away from those things that give false comfort. Help us to be better comforters to others. In Jesus' mighty name. Amen.

Reader Foot Notes

Some days you bloom. Some days you grow roots. Both matter.

Double Blessings

God's Foot Notes

*"Let your light so shine before men,
that they may see your good works and glorify your Father in heaven."*
Matthew 5:16

Author Foot Notes

Isn't it funny how some of us need to learn and repeatedly relearn before we finally understand the meaning behind a lesson?

During a setback due to an unexpected injury, I was reminded of a very valuable lesson of the importance of letting others bless us.

I had suffered a horrible fall that ended up breaking my foot in two places. As an amputee, I only have one foot. Breaking that one foot turned my typically challenging life into serious overdrive. Instantly I was setback a decade. Physically I was back in a wheelchair and home-bound unless I allowed others to help me. Emotionally and mentally, I battled the triggers in my mind that Satan used to try and isolate me into fear and depression. As a limb loss, handicapped individual, I experience the constant battle of finding the healthy balance between doing it myself versus asking someone for help. Both decisions are necessary for success and growth, and neither are particularly easy, especially for someone like me who has an independent streak!

Realizing I would need assistance, I marveled at how God provided helpers in my time of need. Most people I knew. Some I did not know very well at all. I wish I could describe the look on people's faces when they reached out to help me. I could see the priceless joy radiating from their faces. No wonder Jesus taught a great deal about serving others. It makes my heart smile every time I have the opportunity to participate in the process of serving.

At one point in my recovery, I was feeling a bit sorry for myself. I was also physically exhausted from the constant battles of maneuvering life in a wheelchair. The combination of emotional discouragement and physical exhaustion is not a good mix. I wanted to hibernate and retreat into my home. I even began to refuse offers of help. But God spoke kindly to my heart, *Maybe this isn't about you, young lady*. I love how gently and lovingly God addresses our selfish behaviors. He is such a Gentleman!

Don't take away her blessing.

Shortly after my attitude adjustment from God, I received a text from a woman I did not know very well at all. Her message was precious, stating how it would bless her so much if there was something she could do to help me. At that particular time, I did not need a single thing. The house was clean, the groceries were stocked, the errands were run, the mail was brought in, and the laundry was done. In my heart I heard God saying, *Don't take away her blessing*. I replied to the woman's sweet offer of help with, "You are so kind to offer. Thank you. I could use a couple of rolls of toilet paper and a jar of peanut butter the next time you are out. There is no hurry."

Within an hour that sweet woman delivered the toilet paper and peanut butter to my door. She had the biggest smile on her face! She repeatedly thanked me for letting her serve. In that moment, I learned the deeper lesson. I learned it was not about my receiving the blessing but rather not taking away her blessing to serve.

As servants of Jesus Christ - the greatest Servant of all - our primary goal in serving others is to honor Him with our service regardless of what that service is. Whether we are serving others in word or in deed, we are to do it as if we are doing it for God. When we serve with this motive, our efforts take on a much deeper purpose. It becomes a matter of the heart.

When we give Jesus the rightful place in our lives, our love for Him will be shown in our love and service to others. Our primary goal in helping others is to honor Him... regardless of what that task is. Jesus made it perfectly clear when speaking to His disciples - which includes you and me - in Mark 9:35, *"If anyone desires to be first, he shall be last of all and servant of all."* Those last three words hold great significance. Servant of all. Let that sink in a moment. A servant, in biblical terms, is one who sets aside all rights of his own to serve another. The last time I looked, all still means ALL. According to Jesus we are to serve all people. That is certainly a tall order, even for those who are naturally gifted with a servant's heart. In my personal experience the more I intentionally serve others, the greater the desire is to help those in need.

God's Word reminds us that being a Christ-follower will not be easy. Many continue to be persecuted for their faith. So, why do people choose to follow Him despite the mistreatment they will encounter? It's because they know this world is not their forever home.

We are simply passing through, but while we are here, God has called us to love and serve others. I encourage you to ask God how you can grow your servant-heart and honor Him in the process. May we all seek to surrender our selfish pride and replace it with a humble, servant heart.

God may ask you to reach out to someone in need. He may call you to receive help from another who needs to be blessed by giving. We never know when God might use our humility to abundantly bless another!

Foot Notes Application *Date:*

When you serve, are you doing it to honor God or for the praise of others?

What gifts has God given you that you might use to serve others?

What is keeping you from serving others?

Prayer

Heavenly Father,
Thank You for Your Son Jesus - the greatest example of self-sacrifice. May we choose to honor You by serving others. Help us to turn from our selfish pride and seek Your ways. May we love others the way You do. In Jesus' mighty name. Amen.

Reader Foot Notes

A God idea is way better than a good idea.

The Quiet Engineer

God's Foot Notes

"Pray without ceasing."
I Thessalonians 5:17

Author Foot Notes

My first book, *One Foot in Heaven,* had recently released. God graciously brought book sales, a book signing tour, and various speaking events. It was an exciting time of great opportunity to share His story through mine.

A dear friend and podcast host suggested I record an audio version of the book. "You have got to tell your story!" She said. "I would love to, but I do not have the resources for such a costly project," I replied. She and I had just finished recording the second part of a series for her podcast show and her producer overheard us talking. "I can help you out with the audio recording," he said. "Thank you, sir, but I really do not have the finances," I responded. "Look, I think we can work something out. I am in between jobs and am really wanting to break out on my own. I am almost done setting up my recording studio. If you are willing, I would love for your project to be the one I get my feet wet with." He quoted me a price for his time and assured me he was capable of seeing the project through to completion. I later learned the price he quoted me was a fraction of what a main stream recording studio would charge. "I would like to pray about it before I commit. May I call you in a few days?" I asked. "Sure," he replied.

I had only met the sound engineer twice and did not really know anything about him. I reached out to my friend who used his sound engineering for her podcast show. She said he was a good guy and that he was harmless. The later comment was comforting as I learned he was a single man and his recording studio was in his home.

After much prayer and quiet time with God, I believed the recording opportunity was meant to happen and that God would use it to bless others. One of my on-going prayers is that God uses my story of finding hope in the hopeless for the lost and weary souls. Only then will the horrific physical battle I continue to fight be worth it.

I called the recording engineer. We ironed out all of the details. The hardest part for me would be the hour plus drive each way to his studio. We had no idea how many days it would take to record, edit, and re-record the book. He estimated we would be able to do two or three chapters a day in addition to a day or two for edit do-overs. We anticipated a couple of weeks of work ahead of us.

Our first recording day started a bit slow. The engineer had everything set up, but he needed me to go through various items. Did I want him to record the forward? How about chapter titles? What about audio clips for marketing purposes? Did I know how to use the equipment set before me? And, of course, there were numerous sound recording samplers of my voice for necessary pitch, clarity and volume settings. Then there were my legs. Sitting for long periods of time can be a huge physical challenge for me. The first day was nearly half over before we were ready to record the first page.

A heart that chooses God in spite of our circumstances.

"Before we start, I would like to pray," I said. I remember the prayer being one of thanksgiving to God for the opportunity and for favor and blessing for the sound engineer and his new business. I didn't think much of it as I assumed he was a praying man. Or so I thought.

Once I got into a rhythm, reading my story aloud was easy. After all, I was the one who lived it. We paused recording after each chapter so I could stretch my legs. The first day we ended with four chapters recorded. In spite of the delays and training, we were ahead of schedule. I was so excited! I could not help ending our time in prayer - *Thank You Lord!*

Two recording days later I read the closing line. Yes, two days. That in itself was a miracle! Each day the engineer waited patiently as I started and ended each session in prayer. I prayed before he flipped all the buttons on, and I immediately prayed again once he flipped them all off.

The re-recording of edits took a couple more days, but they were short sessions. Yep! I began and completed those days in prayer as well. The recording engineer never said a word. Not even a smile or a nod. He didn't seem phased in the least by all the prayer. I figured if he was upset by it he would have somehow let me know.

Before we started recording the final clip on the last day he said, "I think you need to add something to the audio book. I think you should end with a prayer. It only seems fitting."

"What a GREAT idea!"

The audio version doesn't contain photos like the print or e-version, but it contains something very special to me. A Spirit-led, non-rehearsed, first take prayer for the listener. What a precious ending to the audio book.

On my drive home from our final recording session, I could not stop replaying Mr. Engineer's suggestion of the ending prayer. The entire time I thought he was unaffected by my daily start and stop prayers. We really can not judge a book by its cover. We never know how God is moving in someone's heart.

In the Bible the Apostle Paul teaches that we are to pray without ceasing. What does that really mean? We can not possibly spend all our time on our knees in prayer. Paul meant that we are to have an attitude of prayer. A heart that chooses God in spite of our circumstances. One where we are engaged with God, and where He is involved in all our thoughts and actions. One where we turn our thoughts into prayer and thanksgiving to God. When we find it natural to pray throughout our daily lives, we become more obedient followers of Jesus Christ.

Foot Notes Application   Date:

Is prayer part of your daily life? If not, how can you make it a part of your day?

What is a short prayer you can say out loud? (Try quoting a favorite Bible verse)

List three things you can pray a prayer of thanksgiving to God.

Prayer

Heavenly Father,
Thank You for the avenue of prayer. Thank You that You hear every word we utter. Help us Lord to grow an attitude of prayer and a heart to pray for others. In Jesus' mighty name. Amen.

Reader Foot Notes

Sometimes big things come from small moments.

The Weary Soul Rejoices

God's Foot Notes

"But those who wait on the Lord shall renew their strength; they shall mount up with wings like eagles, they shall run and not be weary, they shall walk and not faint."
Isaiah 40:31

Author Foot Notes

An on-going physical setback had taken it's toll on me. I was quickly approaching a full year of searching and seeking medical healing - all without results. Friends and family continued to pray. My "keep on keeping on" had reached 'E' (for empty). I was not only tired of the fight, I was weary of the battle. You know what I am talking about. If you have lived at all, you have experienced the weight of weariness at some point in your life. It is exhausting.

It was a gorgeous Sunday morning. As I got ready for church, my mind once again battled the on-going circumstances of my current increased physical limitations. Looking into the mirror, I could almost see the cartoon images, from my childhood, of the devil on one shoulder and an angel on the other. As frustration and tears began to fall, I spoke aloud, "Stop! In the name of Jesus, STOP!" Once again, I surrendered my will - my fight.

I sat through the morning worship and the message in my own personal fog. I was physically sitting in church, but nowhere near present. Dragging myself to my car afterward, my conversation with the Lord began. *God, I am so tired of the fight. How much more?*

I drove home via a peaceful country back road. In my heart I heard *Stop! Stop?* I asked. *Yes. Stop.* As I topped the hill, the next driveway happened to be along the side of a pasture I knew well. For years as I would travel past the well-manicured pasture, my heart would expand and my lips would curve upward as I watched the herd of adorable alpacas frolic and play. It was definitely a happy moment anytime I had driven by them.

I pulled onto the dirt and gravel drive next to the pasture. I sat in my car, the window down, the sun shining, and tears puddling in my eyes. The Lord spoke to my heart while I watched the alpacas meander about the serene setting. A peace I had not felt in nearly a year washed over me. I knew in that moment all would be okay. I didn't know how or what that peace would look like, but I knew God had it. I sat there a few minutes longer with my chin on my folded arms leaning on the opened car door window ledge, staring at the precious animals, as the sun warmed my face. From the corner of my eye, I saw something move near the barn across the pasture. It was a man. He was walking towards me. Oh crap! No doubt, he is going to tell me I am trespassing.

BUT GOD.

Then I saw it. From across the pasture, the man waved. Not a 'shoo!' Get outa here kind of wave, but a hello wave. When he got within speaking distance, I kid you not, he invited me to meet, feed, and visit his alpacas.

"Really? Are you sure?" I asked.

"Yes, they're real friendly," he replied.

"I'm an amputee on crutches. I don't want to scare them."

"No worries. I'll get a chair for you and put it in the pasture. I'll get some feed and they'll come to you," he kindly replied. Y'all, that is exactly what happened—and so much more! I spent three hours in the pasture that day. Best therapy ever!

God knew what I needed and when I needed it. Had I not listened to Him when He said stop, had I not obeyed, had I not taken it to God in prayer in the first place, I would still be burdened and broken with the overwhelming weight of weariness. Growing closer to God isn't the result of trying harder, but of surrendering more.

I knew in that moment all would be okay.

This world is tough. Even those who are strong Christ-followers become weak and worn at times. Isaiah 40:31 tells us, *"But those who wait upon the Lord shall renew their strength; they shall mount up with wings like eagles, they shall run and not be weary, they shall walk and not faint."* And while this verse is often quoted, and may even hang on your wall, most of us fail to put much emphasis on the opening of the verse - *those who wait upon the Lord.* Many times we focus on the flying like eagles and running without fainting rather than waiting on the Lord first.

Waiting on the Lord requires us to trust in God, expecting Him to fulfill His promises so we can rise above life's difficulties and distractions. When we trust God, we are better prepared to hear His voice when He speaks to us. Then, and only then, can we soar like an eagle and run without fainting.

The poet Placide Cappeau, who also was an amputee after losing a limb in a gunshot injury, wrote in 1843 the line "the weary soul rejoices" in the now famous Christmas song "O Holy Night". There's another great line in that song, "a thrill of hope".

Thank You Lord for blessing my weary soul with a thrill of hope through a herd of Your beautiful alpaca creatures.

May you, too, be blessed with a thrill of hope today!

Foot Notes Application *Date:*

What has you weary today?

In what ways can you wait upon the Lord to renew your strength?

What do you need to let go of and surrender to God?

Prayer

Heavenly Father,
Thank You Lord for Your promises. For Your strength when we wait upon You. For Your power that never ends, especially when we are weary and worn. Renew us, Lord, as only You can so our weary souls can rejoice with a thrill of hope in You! In Jesus' mighty name. Amen.

Reader Foot Notes

Gratitude changes the perspective.

Ice Cream and a Prayer

God's Foot Notes

"He who has ears to hear, let him hear!"
Matthew 13:9

Author Foot Notes

I had spent the majority of the day working on my next manuscript in my favorite office space, a balcony overlooking the Gulf of America. Creativity poured out as I held my pen and God wiggled it. My brain and my body were both exhausted. One needed a break, and the other needed movement. Typically I travel solo for writing trips, but because I was still in a walking boot from a broken foot, a sweet friend joined me as a driver and helper. She was a God send!

We had dinner out that particular night and wandered through a few shops afterward. My body was grateful for the stretching and movement after sitting all day. On our way back to the condo, we made a last-minute decision to stop at an ice cream parlor. It was a cute place that smelled like cake, candy and ice cream all rolled into one. Adorable, colored table and chair sets were scattered about both inside and out. Obviously it was a hot spot as the long line of customers made its way around the inside of the shop. I was not sure if my legs were up for the challenge of standing on the hard, concrete flooring. My friend, always mindful of my physical difficulties, suggested I sit at one of the tables while she ordered for me. I was about to take her up on her offer when a tug on my heart directed my eyes to the clerk behind the counter. She was small in stature and seemed withdrawn, but yet she hustled about serving the ever-growing line of customers.

There was something about her that spoke to me. She was professional and courteous as she served her patrons, but I saw pain and brokenness in her. I looked about the rather large shop. She was the only one working. Oh dear, God bless her, I thought to myself. No wonder she looks so worn down!

As we slowly inched our way closer and closer to the long row of ice cream cases, the Holy Spirit pierced my heart and my pocketbook. I noticed a tip jar at the end of the counter near the cash register. From time to time, God places it on my heart to financially bless strangers. It's not huge, but the impact - His impact - is made. Most of the time the financial gifts are anonymous, which is my preference, but for some reason, God wanted me to make eye contact with this woman. *She needs to see My love for her*, He said to my heart.

She was a God send!

The clerk totaled my order, and I paid the bill. As she was counting out my change, I pulled a larger bill from my wallet, folded it neatly, and tucked it into my hand. When she handed me my change, I gently touched her hand. I placed the folded bill and a bookmark about my book into her hand. Looking into her eyes I said, "I appreciate you. You are doing such a great job taking care of everyone!" The eyes that looked back at me were sad, and it broke my heart. She was obviously carrying a much heavier load than that of a long line of customers. The corners of her mouth lifted ever so slightly. Never looking at the folded bill I had placed in her hand, she mumbled a thank you and quickly turned to serve the next customer.

The weather was beautiful that night. My friend and I chose to sit outside as we savored our creamy treats. Other patrons sat at nearby tables visiting and enjoying their sweet dairy delights as well. Halfway through the dessert, I felt a gentle touch on my shoulder. The female clerk asked, as she held out the bookmark in her hand, "Is this you?" "Yes ma'am, it is," I replied. With tears in her eyes, she said, "You're an answer to prayer." Rarely do I get to witness one's joy when they discover they have been the recipient of a random act of kindness that God places on my heart. Honestly, I am okay with not knowing. I watched the walls of insecurity and fear collapse around her as she shared her story with me. Her husband suddenly passed a year prior, and she had been living in chaos ever since. She told me she had been asking God what to do? How to live? How to go on? I asked her, "Can I pray for you?" She immediately nodded.

Once again, I reached for this little lamb's hands and prayed over her in Jesus' name. To my surprise after I said AMEN, there were multiple amens that echoed from customers sitting at other tables around us. It was beautiful! I love how God gathers His kids around a hurting soul and makes a way to love on them.

I wasn't her answer to prayer any more than those sitting around us who echoed amen were. We were all conduits, bridges, to help her cross the chasm between her struggle and Jesus. The formerly meek and mild clerk stood a bit taller, and with a wide genuine smile, she wiped her tears. She hugged and thanked me before running back inside the shop.

Did my prayer heal her broken heart? Of course not! I did, however, help her turn it over to the One who can. It is not our job to fix others. Shoot! We can't fix our own messes. What on earth makes us think we can fix someone else's?

God calls us to love one another. Sometimes that love looks like a word of encouragement or a big dose of grace. Sometimes it is patience with the parent of a screaming child in a restaurant. Sometimes it is a generous tip or an interceding prayer. No matter how God uses us: as soil, water, sunlight, or fertilizer - it is our job to be obedient to the call, and let Him do the growing and the healing in others.

Foot Notes Application

Date:

How can you encourage another?

What are some of the signs of a person in need?

How have you prayed for someone who is hurting?

Prayer

Heavenly Father,
Thank You that You are love. You show us love, and You show us how to love. Lord, please give us ears to hear and eyes to see that we may be Jesus to those in need. We love you. In Jesus' name. Amen.

Reader Foot Notes

The motive is love.

The message is the gospel.

The Right Wrong Number

God's Foot Notes

"Fear not, for I am with you; Be not dismayed, for I am your God. I will strengthen you, Yes, I will help you, I will uphold you with My righteous right hand."
Isaiah 41:10

Author Foot Notes

Rrring. Rrring.

I picked up my cell phone to look at the caller ID. I recognized the name that appeared on the screen, but I was hesitant to answer the call. I was busy working on a project and had not spoken to the caller in over a decade. I was ready to let the call roll to voice mail when I felt that familiar still small voice tug on my heart—*answer it*.

"Hello."

"Hi Sheila. This is Lacey."

"Hi Lacey. How are you?"

"I'm so sorry to bother you, but I need your help," she stated.

"I'll do what I can. How can I help?" I replied.

With exhaustion in her voice she said, "I'm okay, but mom isn't doing well at all in hospice. I don't know what to do."

Realizing that she had called the wrong Sheila, I responded with, "Lacey, I believe you meant to call a different Sheila. This is Sheila Fitzgerald."

"Oh, my gosh! I am SO sorry," she replied. "My mom is in the end-of-life stage of hospice and having a really difficult time. I don't know what to do. I thought I was calling Sheila, her nurse. I'm so sorry."

Seizing the opportunity for God's divine appointment, and His creative switch-a-roo of the Sheila contacts on Lacey's phone, I said, "Lacey, I don't believe you called the wrong Sheila. I believe God wants me to pray for you and your mama. May I take a few seconds to pray for y'all?"

Lacey's delayed response was combined with what felt like a sense of relief. I could hear exhaustion in her voice. Whether she realized it or not, Lacey needed to hear that she was not alone in her struggle. *Lord, please give me the words You want her to hear from You* was my silent plea. I sensed I was to focus the prayer around Lacey. I quickly started to pray, thanking God for Lacey's loving heart - a servant heart that was honoring her mother. I thanked God for the bond between mothers and their children; especially the bond between mamas and daughters, and I thanked God for providing caring hospice care for Lacey's beloved mother. I prayed for strength, wisdom, discernment, and grace for Lacey as she helped her precious mama finish the end of her life with grace and dignity. I prayed for peace to blanket both Lacey and her mother as they journeyed together the difficult road ahead of them. I closed the prayer by thanking God for His Son, Jesus Christ, and for Lacey to turn to Him especially now. I heard soft whimpering on the other end of the line. Lacey softly responded with, "Thank you Sheila. I need to go. Take care." The call ended. I do not know what kind of - if any - relationship Lacey had with Jesus. When I knew her more than a decade prior to this event, there was no sign of her having any interest in Jesus Christ.

I put my cell phone down on the table and immediately thanked God. You see, I also was in a season of exhaustion. I had been dealing with a chronic open wound on my residual limb. For more than a month I had been grounded and spent the majority of my time stuck at home because I was unable to wear my prosthetic leg while waiting for my wound to heal. Recovery was not happening on my time table, and the enemy of my soul knew it. Satan did his best to pick and prod me with lies of accusation. *You call yourself a follower of Jesus? Huh! You're no good to anyone with the mess of a body you have!* My mind knew those were deceiving lies from the pit of hell, but it did not keep me from feeling unwanted and unworthy.

> *"May I take a few seconds to pray for y'all?"*

BUT GOD.

God always knows what we need. I have no doubt God orchestrated every step of the wrong Sheila phone call. He knew all along it was the right wrong Sheila. I needed to be needed, and Lacey needed to know she was not alone. It was a definite win-win Jesus encounter. In my season of poor pitiful Sheila, God used my heart's desire to love on others through prayer to bring me out of the funk I had allowed myself to get into. I pray the boost I received, by praying for another in need, was also a boost Lacey received in her time of need.

    Many times, we, as Christ-followers, are given a mere blink in time to shine Jesus to the world. It could be that simple gesture when we let someone go ahead of us in the grocery line, a polite wave letting a car turn in front of us, a compassionate smile for a mom who is struggling with an overly tired baby, or simply holding a door for someone. I looked back at my phone records and saw that the right, wrong Sheila phone call literally lasted two minutes. Two minutes is .001 percent of a day. Think how amazing this is! When God is involved, He can make an incredible impact in our lives with such a tiny nugget of time. Imagine how miraculous our lives would be if we allowed God to use us for one whole percent of our day!

Foot Notes Application

Date:

What struggles do you need God to help you with? Selfishness? Pride? Guilt? Shame? Fear?

How are you allowing God access to your everyday life?

How can you serve self less and others more?

Prayer

Heavenly Father,
Thank You for the miracles You perform in our lives with the limited, nano-seconds we give you. Father, please forgive us for being so selfish with our time. Help us to surrender to Your will for our lives, and may we walk in Your freedom and on Your timeline. In Jesus' mighty name. Amen.

Reader Foot Notes

God, get into my head before I do.

A Mighty - Albeit - Tiny - Healer

God's Foot Notes

"Therefore comfort each other and edify one another, just as you also are doing."
I Thessalonians 5:11

Author Foot Notes

When I was a teenager, I shared my deepest secrets with our beloved family pet, Gretchen. She was the sweetest, smartest, and most loyal canine companion during my troubled and trying years of youth. If she could have talked, oh my, the stories she would have told!

Although she was petite for the blue heeler breed, she had a strength and character that rivaled the breed standard. Gretchen was a rescue so we really did not know exactly how old she was. The best we could tell she lived more than 20 years. She was the first of five Australian cattle dogs I had in my life. They are incredible dogs.

One of my favorite childhood photos is that of she and I, me barefoot, sitting in the sun with her on my lap. In the photo it looks like I am holding her, but the truth was - she was holding me. As far as I know, it is the only photo I have of me barefoot and still having both feet. It is a cherished treasure.

For months, I struggled with an on-going problem with the knee of my short leg. Eventually I found out the cause of the pain and that the probable solution was another surgery. Ugh! I needed another surgery on these legs like I need another hole in my head. As with any surgery, there are pros and cons. All the standard risks become major when it comes to surgical procedures on an amputated limb. Mentally and emotionally processing all the physical stuff can take its toll; not to mention, the complete starting over of adjusting, and eventually learning how to walk again with a new prosthetic, post surgery, can be exhausting.

It was in those times of great trial that I missed my little support animal Daisy. She was my previous beloved pet who never left my side during the years of recovery after my accident. That was also the first time in more than 50 years that I had not had a dog in my life. That in itself was a huge adjustment. I missed Daisy holding me, leaning her little heart against mine, and not letting go until I was fully consoled. She knew. She ALWAYS knew. Whether it was physical or emotional pain...she knew.

After receiving the news I would most likely need another surgery, I could not stop the tears. Tears of frustration. Tears of anger. Tears of grief. Tears of pain. The hardest tears were those of *How much more Lord?* I cried. I prayed. The more I cried, the more I prayed. The more I prayed, the more cried. I had no more tears. I had no more words to pray. In that moment, all I wanted was that which I no longer had—my beloved Daisy to hold me. She was never bothered by my snot-blowing tears. Instead she would gently place her little snout at my eyes and breath in as if to say, *I see you. I feel your pain.* Then, with great intention, she would deliberately bury her head against my heart and stay there until my hurts were healed. It was a gift like none other.

> *The more I cried, the more I prayed.*

The morning after my latest cry-fest, I went to church early, as I often do, to pray. Once again, the cycle from the previous day continued: more tears, more prayers, repeat. As folks started to arrive, I saw him. I caught my breath as the tears puddled in my heart and seeped out my eyes. A kind young man was carrying a new pup. As he made his way towards me, all I could think was *Oh, Daisy, I miss you!* The young man knelt beside me with the pup in his arms. I gave the backside of my hand to the little canine's nose and introduced myself. The pup pushed himself up in his owner's arms, extending his precious little face towards mine. I longed for a face full of puppy kisses. God knew exactly what my heart needed in that moment. As tears spilled from my eyes, the pup gently reached up and lightly breathed in my tears - first one eye then the other. Never once did he kiss my face or lick my tears. Instead he felt my pain and kissed my heart just like my precious little Daisy used to do and like sweet Gretchen did in my youth. My heart spoke, *God you are SO good!*

The young man, an amazing warrior for Jesus, did not say a word. He did something greater. Tucking his new little pup under one arm, he hugged me. Correct that. It was more than a hug — it was a hold that helped heal my hurting heart. Like his pup, he saw my pain.

I do not know if animals can be anointed by God. What I do know, and scripture confirms it with a talking donkey, that God can and does use animals for His purpose. Just as God used my little Daisy, God used the little pup and his owner when I so desperately needed it. Not a word was necessary.

God sees YOU. He sees when you are hurting. He sees your pain. He hears your prayers. He knows what you need and when you need it. I love God's word in Isaiah 41:10, *"Fear not, for I am with you; be not dismayed for I am your God. I will strengthen you, yes, I will help you, I will uphold you with My righteous right hand."*

By the way, it is not a misprint in the title. I was not sure of the pup breed when I first met him, as he was white brindle in color. When the young man told me his new pup was a blue heeler, I quickly responded by spelling blue h-e-a-l-e-r. The young man looked at me a bit strange as he thought about it. He then replied, "I believe it's spelled h-e-e-l-e-r." To which I responded, "Not this one. This one is definitely a healer."

Isn't it amazing how much God loves us? He combined the breed from the dog of my youth with the precious traits of my beloved Daisy to help heal my hurting heart. ONLY GOD!

Foot Notes Application

Date:

What is burdening your heart?

How is/has God healed your burdened heart?

In what ways can you be more aware of those around you who are hurting?

Prayer

Heavenly Father,
Thank You for Your beloved creatures. Thank You Lord for the comfort of others. Help heal our burdened hearts. May we be aware of those who are hurting, and may we help bring comfort to their pain. In Jesus' mighty name. Amen.

Reader Foot Notes

What I want, what I think, and what I feel does not override God's Word.

Big Hair Brave Heart

God's Foot Notes

*"For I know the plans I have for you," declares the Lord,
"plans to prosper you and not to harm you, plans to give you hope and a future."*
Jeremiah 29:11 NIV

Author Foot Notes

His name was Jeremy. He was small of stature and rather skinny, but his hair was huge! So was his heart and love for his country.

I had stopped by a local retail market to pick up a few greeting cards. I had planned a quick in-and-out, but I soon realized God had other plans in mind. There were a few customers ahead of me at the checkout lane. I spent the time waiting and, as I often do, observing those around me. I watched the young clerk politely ring up each customer's order. It was refreshing to see a young person exhibit kind manners and quality communication.

When it was my turn to pay for the items I'd selected, I took a closer look at the big-haired young man standing before me. As I studied his features, I thought to myself, *I know a lot of women who would love to have his beautiful locks!* He and I exchanged pleasantries. He asked me if I found everything I was looking for and as I replied affirmatively, I continued the conversation by complimenting his hair.

Then it happened. That moment when God connects two strangers.

Jeremy - according to his name tag - looked at me as both of his hands reached for the mounds of curls covering the top of his head. I knew that look. The look that says, *there is way more to this story.* "I don't normally grow it this long, but it's all going to be buzzed off soon."

Again his eyes said more, so I asked, "Will you be serving our military?"

"Yes, ma'am!" he replied as he patriotically touched his right hand to his heart. "I've completed and signed all the paperwork." *He has the heart of a soldier,* I thought to myself.

"Jeremy, thank you! I'm so proud of you! You have no idea what it does for my heart to see a fine young man willing to honor and serve our country." He briefly blushed and responded with another, "Thank you, ma'am."

Though the sales process was completed, I sensed God was not yet done. I glanced behind me and thought to myself, *That's strange. In all the years I have shopped at this store, I have never, not once, had no customers waiting behind me in the checkout lane.*

"What would you like to learn in the military?" I asked.

Jeremy's eyes lit up. "I wanna fly planes."

Seeing the joy in his eyes, I said, "Jeremy, that's awesome! My brother is a pilot and he loves it! I think you're going to be an excellent pilot!"

Under his breath, Jeremy tentatively replied, "I hope so."

Despite his joy his eyes began to look less confident and uncertain.

"Have you flown a plane before?" I asked. "Do you have your private pilot's license?"

"No, ma'am. Not yet. But I've been up (in a plane) a lot. I love it! It's so peaceful soaring up above the clouds." Suddenly, although I wasn't sure why, Jeremy's entire countenance changed.

"I'm a little bit afraid," he admitted.

"I think that's a very healthy response, Jeremy. It would be unrealistic for you not to be somewhat afraid."

"It is better to give than receive."

Jeremy countered by saying, "Oh, I'm not afraid to fly." Then he proceeded to share his fear of being gone from home for so long. By his calculations he could easily be gone for six or more years. The uncertainty of his committed future played havoc with his mind.

"When do you leave for bootcamp?" I asked.

Jeremy didn't know the exact date, but I knew I'd hit a tender spot with my last question.

Silently, I thanked God for this brave-hearted young man and asked the Lord to give me the right words to speak to him. I do not recall the exact words of encouragement God gave me, but I do remember the giant smile on Jeremy's face and a spirit of calm that came over him. Standing tall, his shoulders back, and with that big bushy head of bouncing curls, Jeremy grinned as he thanked me for the confidence boost.

"You've got this," I said. "More importantly, God's got YOU, Jeremy."

Feeling God's peace of completion, I grabbed my bag and turned to leave.

I've been in that store nearly every week for the past seven years, and there is always a line of customers behind me. I had never seen Jeremy before that day, and I have yet to see him since. Maybe he was filling in from another store? I believe God planned for Jeremy to be at that location and at that time for our chance encounter. A Divine appointment, you might say.

I know God has blessed me with the gift of exhortation, and I have always loved encouraging others. But I admit that there are times I don't recognize it when God is calling me to serve someone with His words. Like anything else, it takes practice. Actually it takes more than practice. It takes faithful obedience. Some days I am more obedient to His calling than other days. Aren't we all? Have you noticed that the greatest joy comes when we're faithfully obedient to His callings? I easily could have ignored Jeremy and not engaged in conversation with him. Think of what I would have missed! The joy that comes from serving others is ah-mazing! The old saying is true, "It is better to give than receive." My prayer is that we all do more of it.

Let us end with where we began: with the familiar verse in Jeremiah 29:11, "*God knows the plans He has for us.*" Not only for the big-haired, brave-hearted Jeremy, but for you as well my friend. *"Then you will call on Me and come and pray to Me, and I will listen to you." (Says the Lord)* Jeremiah 29:12.

Foot Notes Application   Date:

What are some fears you have that are holding you back?

Have you shared those fears with Jesus?

In what tangible ways can you overcome those fears?

Prayer
Father God,
Thank You for loving us so much that You tell us often in Your Holy Word that we are not to be afraid. Help us Lord when we are fearful and help us to turn to You when we are. In Jesus' mighty name. Amen.

Reader Foot Notes

*If the enemy can not stop you

he will insult you.*

Hallway Heartbreak

God's Foot Notes

"Set your mind on things above, not on things on the earth."
Colossians 3:2

Author Foot Notes

 Years ago I was asked to speak to a group of healthcare providers. The conference room was filled with men and women who were from various places across the state of Tennessee. I shared my testimony of *One Foot in Heaven* and did my best to acknowledge and encourage the medical professionals seated before me. I wanted them to know through my message that what they did in their daily practice mattered and what a huge difference they make in the lives of their patients.

 I have learned over the years how to read the room and respond accordingly. Because the audience was full of medical professionals, I knew I needed to be real, raw, and focus on the details of my physical journey and years of recovery from severe physical trauma. The conference attendees, who rarely experienced the patient side of life after trauma, were fully engaged - especially the men. *Interesting* I thought to myself.

 I received a very kind and unexpected standing ovation. I wasn't certain how to respond! Tears filled my eyes as I humbly thanked them and gave glory to God.

 At the conclusion of my speaking events, I routinely remain available for questions or comments from the audience. Some attendees want photographs or a private one-on-one conversation. After completing my session, I gathered my things and prepared to leave. I exited the conference room through a side door used only by the presenters. Upon entering the quiet, rather dark hallway, I paused long enough to thank God and to gently exhale from the excitement I had just experienced on the other side of that door.

The long hallway was empty as the next conference session had started. I repositioned my shoulder bag of materials, then I looked up and noticed someone at the other end of the hallway walking toward me. It was a man. I noticed he had a unique gait. Then I saw it. He, too, was an amputee. As he got closer to me, I recognized his face. During my presentation I noticed his head nodding in agreement from time to time, but he rarely looked up at me.

As he approached me, he immediately apologized for not speaking to me in the conference room. He was afraid to. He introduced himself as Nathan. He was kind, gentle, and gracious as he thanked me for sharing what he called "the really hard stuff about being an amputee." With his head hung low, he shared how hard it was for him to work in the healthcare arena as an amputee.

I sensed there was more Nathan wanted to tell me...so I waited patiently for him to speak. He lifted his face toward mine, and with tear-filled eyes the grown man before me spent the next several minutes pouring his heart out to me. As he spoke, I silently prayed, *Oh, Lord, help me comfort this burdened man. Give me Your words, please.* Nathan shared the weight of what he felt as his colleagues relied on him to know-it-all when it came to everything amputation - as if every limb loss patient is exactly the same. Not. At. All. There are numerous variables in any amputation, and it is unreasonable to compare one patient to another. Nathan tearfully continued to share the pressure he'd put on himself to be everything his colleagues and patients expected him to be, even though he knew it was both illogical and impossible.

Then I saw it.

For those who have experienced near-death trauma, it is common that they question, "Why am I still alive?" Many people who have a NDE (near death experience) struggle with survivor's guilt and feel pressured that they were spared for a bigger purpose. These survivors spend the rest of their lives either chasing the bigger purpose, or becoming burdened by the weight of the expectations of others. Nathan was living the burdened path.

My new amputee friend continued to share his struggles with me by telling me how hard it is to feel that he has to prove himself to family and friends. The exhausting mental battles impact the quality of his sleep - a commodity amputees desperately need. I understood exactly where Nathan was coming from. For years, I heard people say, "God saved you. He must have something really big for you to do."

I placed the shoulder bag I had been carrying on the floor and repositioned my feet - something lower limb amputees do a lot! The next thing I knew, I was cradling Nathan's head on my shoulder as he cried tears of heartache, frustration and pain. I held the hurting soul until his shoulders lowered in surrender and his tears ran dry. Nathan slowly stepped back. He thanked me repeatedly for sharing, listening, caring, and as he said, "getting it". As I watched my new friend walk away, I noticed he stood a bit taller, he held his head higher, and the unique gait I saw the first time I encountered him had morphed into a confident swagger. *Thank You Lord!*

    We all place unrealistic expectations on ourselves and on one another. These cause heartache and failure, both of which make Satan smile. I don't know about you, but making Satan happy is not on my radar! When our hearts are set on the things of man - unrealistic expectations - and not on God, we become stumbling blocks to ourselves and to others. When we set our hearts on God, we can rest in His love, His plan and, His acceptance. I love what Paul wrote in Colossians 3:16, *"Let the word of Christ dwell in you richly in all wisdom, teaching and admonishing one another in psalms and hymns and spiritual songs, singing with grace in your hearts to the Lord."*

Foot Notes Application   Date:

Why do we place unrealistic expectations on ourselves and on others?

In what ways can you give yourself grace?

What are some ways you can grant others grace?

Prayer

Heavenly Father,
Thank You for loving us, especially when we find it hard to love ourselves. Lord, please show us how to set our thoughts on You and not get burdened by unrealistic expectations for ourselves and for others. May we grant grace in love. We love You! In Jesus' mighty name. Amen.

Reader Foot Notes

There is mercy in suffering.

Baker's Dozen

God's Foot Notes

"Does He not see my ways, and count all my steps?"
Job 31:4

Author Foot Notes

September 29th was quickly approaching. As I do every year, I pray for a fun, positive way to celebrate the annual date of the accident that forever changed my life. Unbeknown to me God had much bigger plans for anniversary number twelve than I did.

I was scheduled to speak at a crusade event outside Tampa, Florida. The 29th happened to fall on my travel day. I knew it would be a long, busy, and most-likely challenging day for me. Knowing it would be a difficult day, I asked God for His blessings. Simple ease for my travel day was the best way I thought to celebrate the twelfth anniversary. I chose to conquer the flight, rental car, and all logistics without an assistant—even though I was still ambulating via crutches.

My day began with a 3am wake-up call. Nine hours later I was settled into the hotel room with my legs up. My body was exhausted and grateful for the respite. As my weary body slowly started to unwind and relax, I thought over the day - giving thanks to God for His protection and provision every step of the way. My mind wandered through the various encounters I had with strangers along my journey from Tennessee to Florida. One after another, God placed kind, helpful folks throughout my day.

As I often do, I grabbed a pen and paper and began compiling a list of all those who graciously served my needs. For grins, I counted the people on my list—12. That's so cool! The Lord crossed my path with 12 individuals who chose to give kindness to a stranger on the 12th anniversary of the accident. I sat back and closed my eyes. I prayed for each one on the list that God would bless them abundantly for their kindness to one in need (me).

The next thing I knew, I'd awakened from a 20 minute crash nap. You know, the kind of cat nap you don't remember ever closing your eyes in the first place. The list of strangers was still in my lap. I glanced back through it. *Oh my gosh! I can't believe I forgot Pastor and Mrs Henry.* In my exhausted stupor I had failed to include the most impactful couple I encountered that day.

Unbeknown to me God had much bigger plans.

Earlier that day I had driven the rental car to pick up a few snacks and a case of bottled water for the weekend. Upon returning to the hotel, I somehow managed while on crutches to push a luggage cart to the car in order to haul the case of water to my hotel room. I opened the back hatch on the rental SUV when I heard a kind voice say, "Can we help you with that?" I looked up to see a sweet couple walking towards me. The fella handed his cup of tea to his bride as they walked closer. Me? I was clumsily still trying to figure out how to hold the luggage cart from rolling away all while maneuvering about on crutches.

The kind gentleman stepped in and quickly helped this goofy girl in distress. He noticed stacks of my books and inquired. That was the start of a lovely conversation in the hotel parking lot. Pastor Henry and his sweet Mrs. traveled to Florida from New Jersey to celebrate their retired pastor's 80th birthday. I also learned that the birthday boy appointed my new friend, Mr Henry, as his replacement pastor once he retired. It was a bit of a shock to Mr Henry, and most of the congregation, as they expected another gentleman to be selected for the position. I could sense some anxiousness and apprehension from Mr and Mrs Henry when they spoke about it. Apparently the other man might be in town for the birthday celebration as well.

The Holy Spirit tugged on my heart to pray for them, right then and there. Mr Henry held one of my hands and his bride held my other hand. I do not recall the prayer as it wasn't for me, but for them. I do remember praying that if the man who was not given the pastorship chose to attend the party that a beautiful, peaceful, rekindling of friendship between Mr Henry and him would be healed and that the birthday celebration would be the clean-slate start for them to both move forward. Pastor Henry prayed for me and the crusade and all it entailed.

As the three of us echoed amen in unison, I noticed a man 6-8 parking spaces away from where we were. He was intently watching us. Pastor Henry looked at me then turned to look in the direction I was looking. Mr Henry whispered, "Oh my. That's the other pastor who's position was given to me." All I could do was smile and say, "God is so good. He's already setting His plan in motion."

   Mr and Mrs Henry were so kind to help me get the luggage cart loaded, into the hotel, and on to the elevator. When they got off the elevator for their floor, we said our bless-filled goodbyes. As the elevator door slowly closed, I heard Pastor Henry, in a loud exuberant voice yell, "WOW!"

   In my post cat nap stupor I had completely forgotten about meeting Mr and Mrs Henry. I picked up the list from my lap and counted the names once again. It was no longer 12. The list contained 13 random strangers whom God placed in my life to help me on a very special day. A baker's dozen. With God the gifts are always more—ABUNDANTLY more. *"I have come that they may have life, and that they may have it more abundantly."* John 10:10b.

Foot Notes Application

Date:

How and where is God directing your steps?

Is there an unresolved relationship in your life?

Pray and ask God how to walk out the steps of reconciliation.

Prayer
Heavenly Father,
Thank You for Your guidance in our lives. Please bring reconciliation to our conflicts. Help us to be more aware of Your plans and to be willing to follow You. In Jesus' mighty name Amen.

Reader Foot Notes

You can not be joyful without gratitude.

My Beloved Favorite

God's Foot Notes

"Cast all your care upon Him, for He cares for you."
I Peter 5:7

Author Foot Notes

Have you ever had one of those stirrings in your heart that you know is not of your own doing? For months, every single day, someone I know who does not live near me tip-toed across my heart. Every time the same message. I knew I could not put it off any longer. God was definitely calling me to reach out to them. The greater question...Would I obey?

I sent the letter below to a dear loved one. As I was writing it, God clearly showed me I needed to share it with our hurting world.

The letter may be for you personally. The letter may be for you to share with another. The letter may be a draft for you to modify for your own particular heart stirring. However you choose to receive it, I pray you are ultimately, and abundantly blessed.

Dear Beloved Favorite,

You have been heavy on my heart for a very long time. I know who put you there...God did. I have prayed fervently about how to respond to that heart call. Please forgive me for my selfish lack in not writing sooner. I also pray you will forgive me for not knowing the answer to that which tugs my soul.

Do you know Jesus? Really know Him? Have you chosen Him as the Lord and Savior of your life? Do you have a relationship with Him? Or is your knowledge of Jesus simply a manmade, check-the-

box, token religious practice of maybe thinking about God on random Christian holidays or when you step into a church building for a wedding or a funeral?

Have you ever wondered, "What happens next? When I die, then what?" We all have those thoughts, you know.

God's Holy Word, the Bible, tells us when we die there are only two options as to where we will spend eternity. One, with Jesus in Heaven. Or, heaven forbid, a life of eternal suffering in hell.

For me personally, I have endured horrific torment, pain, and suffering in this life. There is no way I would even consider risking a life like that of eternity in hell.

I have also experienced the supernatural, miraculous presence of Jesus. There is nothing greater. Absolutely NOTHING! If you have never experienced Him, I challenge you to ask God for it. Ask Him to show Himself to you. He wants to do just that. He is a gentleman. He will not force Himself on you, and neither will I. The invitation is your choice and yours alone.

Giving your life to God is not a check-the-box set of rules. It is a heart matter. God knows your heart. Shoot, He even knows before you know if you will give your heart to and follow Him. In some way, it is like any relationship gone awry. You share with God that you recognize all you have done wrong. You own (confess) your mistakes and failures (sin). You ask God for forgiveness. You ask for His help as you make a promise to God to stop doing (repent) those sinful things. You thank God for sending His only Son, Jesus, to die as a sacrifice for your sins. A free gift of eternal salvation for the asking. You can walk in freedom knowing you have been forgiven and freely choose to follow Jesus by following Gods word (Bible).

Will you answer the call?

Only you and God truly know your heart. And just in case you are thinking, "Yeah, but you don't know all I have done. There is no way God would ever forgive me." There is nothing He can't forgive. Trust Him. Believe Him. The freedom in releasing a life of the burden of sin?...Priceless. Eternally priceless!

Because I love God and because I adore you, I can't not share that which I know. If you found an amazing restaurant that completely changed the joy of food for you, wouldn't you be telling everyone? You would be posting photos and sharing it with the world. You, my beloved favorite, are WAY more important than food!

I don't know your heart. You do and God certainly does. My desire for you, my beloved favorite, is the same as Jesus' desire for you, "For this is the will of my Father, that everyone who looks on the Son and believes in Him should have eternal life, and I will raise him up on the last day." John 6:40

I certainly do not claim to have all the answers—hardly! But I know Who does, and I am more than happy to walk the journey of discovering them together with you, my beloved favorite.

You, my beloved favorite, are SO loved!

No doubt as you were reading the letter above, there was as least one person who came to your mind. If you are like most of us, you could make a list of several names. As you read the letter again, create a list of the names God places upon your heart. Next, pray for all the individuals on the list, asking God to show you how you can be His salt and light to them. Ask Him which people on your list He wants you to specifically engage with. Whether they are non-believers or back-slidden Christians who need help finding their way back to Jesus, all are precious to God. God is calling you to walk in His faithful obedience. Will you answer the call?

Foot Notes Application   Date:

Read the sample letter above asking God to help you make a list of those who He is calling you to reach out to.

Pray specifically asking God to show you how you can help those on your list.

In what ways can you be salt and light to those on your list?

Prayer

Heavenly Father,
Thank You for Your incredible adventures with Jesus. Help us to be more aware of the everyday encounters with Jesus. May we remove our blinders and distractions and seek to serve You as You bring opportunities for us to be Your salt and light. In Jesus' mighty name. Amen.

Reader Foot Notes

The worst sin? Being a slave to it.

Conclusion

Come Home to Jesus

Do you know Jesus Christ as your personal Lord and Savior? Did you once call on Jesus but have turned away from Him?

It is not too late to come home to Jesus for the first time nor is it too late to run back home to Jesus if you have strayed away. God's Word tells us in Romans 3:23 that all have sinned. No matter how kind and moral we might be, we are still sinners. Sin is what keeps us apart from God and apart from an eternal life in Heaven with Him. According to the Bible there are only two options for where we will spend life after death; Heaven or Hell.

God is righteous, holy, and perfect, which means one must be perfect to be in His presence. The *only* way for us to be cleansed of our sin, so we can spend eternity with God, is by the free gift of Jesus' blood - the blood He willingly gave on the cross. The gift is free, but we must receive it. God is a Gentleman. He will not force anyone to take the gift His Son Jesus gave. That is called free will. God is offering. Will you take it?

Choosing to make Jesus the Lord and Savior of your life is a decision only you can make. The Bible tells us that if we confess and repent of our sins, believe Jesus is the Son of God, that He died for our us, and that He overcame death by rising from the grave, we will be saved. If there is a stirring in your heart, that is the Holy Spirit calling you to Jesus. Answer the call. Talk to Him today. Say yes to Jesus!

Now, go be intentional. Get connected to a Bible-teaching church, make a public confession of your faith by baptism, read your Bible daily, and spend quality time in prayer. Being a Christ-follower is not always easy, but it will be the greatest adventure of your life!

Practical Ways to Increase Your Salt and Light

* PRAY

* Be in the Word everyday. If you find that daunting, start with reading a version of the Bible that you will commit to reading.

* Practice being intentionally kind to strangers. Soon it will become a habit.

* Greet others with a smile. It too will become a habit.

* LOOK UP! Many times we miss God's opportunities because we are distracted by our devices.

* Say hello. Most of the time, all it takes is a simple hello to begin a conversation.

* Send a text of encouragement: *thinking about you, praying for you, grateful for you, God bless you.* The 15 seconds of your time is truly rewarding!

* Mail a note or card. Yes, it is *old school,* but that is exactly why it so memorable to the recipient.

* Ask restaurant servers, *We will be praying for our meal. How can we pray for you?* If you are not yet comfortable with public prayer, start with your family as you join one another around the table.

* Write an encouraging word on the receipt when you sign the bill.

* Copy or create your own version of *My Beloved Favorite* letter and mail or email it to loved ones who have wandered away or do not yet know Jesus.

* Compliment strangers with genuine compliments.

* Always practice the Golden Rule.

* Pray with your spouse, friends, neighbors, coworkers.

* Pray with the children in your life.

* Teach your children to pray. Keep it simple: "Thank You, God, for _____. Please help_____. In Jesus' name. Amen." Make it a daily practice at the dinner table and at bedtime.

* Read the Bible to your children. Let them read a children's Bible to you.

* Engage with others by volunteering your time at local shelters or charity events.

The best place to practice being salt and light is in our own homes. Soon it will become a family affair!

We must be the salt in order to shine the light

Coming Soon

FootNotes
Adventures With Jesus

VETERANS EDITION

A 30-Day Journaling Devotional

Encountering Jesus on the Battlefields of Life

Sheila Preston Fitzgerald

by
Sheila Preston Fitzgerald

One Foot in Heaven

Finding Hope in the Hopeless

A Miraculous True Story

Supernatural Rescue. Severe Suffering. Mind-blowing Resilience. Endless Inspiration.

A tragic near-death accident turns triumphant and even joy-filled as the God of Grace pours His lavish love on Sheila Preston Fitzgerald, a Southern belle who brings her tenacious, can-do spirit to the fight for her life.

While several years of tremendous pain, multiple surgeries, daily physical therapy, and the ever-present risk for serious setbacks take a toll on all aspects of Sheila's life, her grit to go on, her passion for life, and the above-and-beyond love of her "village" of friends encourage everyone she encounters.

Join Sheila as she recounts her heartfelt—at times horrific, at times hilarious—journey. From one night that changed everything to her spiritual healing with the Savior, Sheila passes along incredible hope as she walks with One Foot in Heaven.

One Foot in Heaven is available on Amazon, Kindle, and where books are sold. Audio version is available on Audible, and read by the author.

Sheila Preston Fitzgerald
Author ~ Speaker
Tragedy Coach

Sheila Preston Fitzgerald is alive today only by the Grace of God. A near-death motorcycle accident that should have taken her life, instead, filled this Godly woman with a passion larger than life itself. Sheila's love of people, love of life, and most importantly her love for Jesus, radiates in all she does. Her miraculous testimony of redemptive healing, from the inside out, will have you laughing and crying with joy. In spite of multiple horrific losses and countless "one step forward - two steps back" do-overs, Sheila has learned to, literally, walk out her incredible journey of faith and recovery.

Sheila's first book One Foot in Heaven is the miraculous true story of finding hope in the hopeless. She is a passionate public speaker who brings hope to any audience. She has appeared on numerous TV, video, and podcast shows shining the light of Jesus to the world.

Sheila pours her heart into prayer, loves all things pen and paper, relishes time with friends, and is an avid fan of God's glorious sunlight especially on the beach. She writes devotion blogs and continues to work on more books in the Foot Notes devotional books series. Sheila resides south of Nashville Tennessee with her beloved pup, Ivy, where she loves to connect with readers.

www.SheilaPrestonFitzgerald.com
Facebook: Sheila Preston Fitzgerald
Instagram: 1FootInHeaven

Made in the USA
Middletown, DE
23 July 2025